Jacob of Sarug's Homily Concerning the Red Heifer and the Crucifixion of our Lord

Texts from Christian Late Antiquity

78

Series Editor

George Anton Kiraz

TeCLA (Texts from Christian Late Antiquity) is a series presenting ancient Christian texts both in their original languages and with accompanying contemporary English translations.

Jacob of Sarug's Homily Concerning the Red Heifer and the Crucifixion of our Lord

Edited and Translated by

Demetrios Alibertis

GORGIAS PRESS

2022

Gorgias Press LLC, 954 River Road, Piscataway, NJ, 08854, USA

www.gorgiaspress.com

2022

ISBN 978-1-4632-4471-2   ISSN 1935-6846

Library of Congress Cataloging-in-Publication Data

A Cataloging-in-Publication Record is available from the Library of Congress.

Printed in the United States of America

TABLE OF CONTENTS

INTRODUCTION

INFORMATION ON THIS HOMILY

Homily Title: Concerning the Red Heifer which is commanded in the Law to be burnt in place of the sins of the assembly: And concerning the Crucifixion of our Lord.

Source of Text: *Homiliae Selectae Mar-Jacobi Sarugensis*, edited by Paul Bedjan (Paris-Leipzig: Harrassowitz, 1907, 2nd ed. Piscataway: Gorgias Press, 2006), vol. 3, pp. 242–259. [Homily 77]

Lines: 344

In his seventy-seventh *mimrō*, Jacob of Sarug expounds on one of the most intriguing and puzzling sacrifices commanded in the Hebrew Bible, the red heifer slaughter ritual in Numbers 19. In this rite, the Israelites were instructed to take a perfect, unblemished, red heifer, upon which no yoke was ever laid, and to deliver it to the priest who would remove it from the camp. Outside of the camp, the heifer was slaughtered before the priest who would, thereafter, take some of the blood and sprinkle it towards the entrance of the Tent of Meeting, seven times. After the sprinkling of the blood, the entire animal, was completely immolated. The priest, as instructed, threw into the great conflagration which consumed the heifer three items – cedar wood, hyssop and a piece of wool material dyed scarlet. At the end of this process, the ashes of the animal were collected by an individual who was ritually pure and were stored in a clean place to be used by the Israelites to purify themselves and their dwellings from corpse impurity. Jacob examines all aspects of the brief chapter, but focuses especially on the enigma of the ritual; while the ashes of the red heifer were supposed to have a purga-

1

tive effect and, as such, were to be used to expunge impurity from those who had come into contact with a corpse or grave, all involved in the sacrifice itself were rendered unclean by it for the duration of the day. The officiating priest and all other participants were permitted to re-enter the camp of the Israelites in the evening, only after having washed their clothing and having bathed themselves. It is on this very puzzling and contradictory situation that Mar Jacob is able to skillfully weave together a typological interpretation of the narrative, portraying every feature of the ritual as being a type (*tupsō*), or a symbol (*rōzō*), or a shadow (*ṭelōnitō*) that depicts (*ṣōar*) Christ's passion, blood and death. For Jacob, the entire story is a prefigurement of Christ's death and its ability to restore and permanently purify all who enter the church through baptism.

Jacob's *mimrō 'On the Red Heifer'* consists of 172 stanzas written in dodecasyllabic meter and was divided into ten sections by Bedjan in his critical edition.[1] In section 1 (lines 1–36), Jacob begins with a rhetorical preamble in which he declares his inability to approach the subject matter. He begins by stating how he is approaching the treasury of God's mysteries to make trade with it (*lmettagōru*). Jacob requests that God give him the ability to understand the many symbols of the narrative and he, in turn, will reveal the mysteries to his audience. There are three interconnected elements in this introductory section which are notable. First, Jacob claims that that the Son of God is alluded to many times in Moses' writings, and how the mystery of the crucifixion and the image of Christ's death are portrayed through the medium of the various sufferings portrayed in Scripture (15–16; 19–30). Second, Jacob claims that it is only through divine revelation that one can comprehend the meaning

---

[1] Bedjan based his edition on two manuscripts: (a) London, British Library, Add. 14,725, f. 29ᵃff; (b) Oxford, Bodleian Library, Cat. 135 (= Pococke 404), f. 379ᵃff. See Paulus Bedjan, ed., *Homiliae Selectae Mar-Jacobi Sarugensis*, (vol. 3; Paris-Leipzig 1905; 2nd ed. Piscataway: Gorgias Press, 2006), V-XIV.

of Scriptures (3–6; 9–14; 17–18). Finally, the element of the Eucharist is brought into the introduction and is portrayed, albeit somewhat cryptically at this point, as being the true source of understanding (5–8; 17–18). It is only later in the *mimrō* that a typological association will be made between the ritual and the Eucharist.

Section 2 (lines 37–66) begins by depicting Moses as an artist who used choice pigments of prophecy (*gawne gbayō danbiutō*) to depict Christ throughout the Scriptures (37–38). Jacob claims that the blood sacrifices of the Hebrew Bible prepared the road of the crucifixion and honored the great slaughter of Christ that was to tread on the same path (39–42). Jacob sees the cross of Jesus and the crucifixion prefigured (*metnaṣar*) in all the sin-offerings involving blood in Scripture, especially as the blood of the animal, such as that of the heifer, had the ability to atone one from sin and to purify the elect of God (41–48). Jacob finishes the section by warning his audience that if they are attached to worldly possessions and do not approach the story in love, they will neither be able to understand the symbols nor see the hidden things therein. One must be fully immersed in love for God and lean towards God, in order for them to understand the mysteries depicted (49–64).

Section 3 (lines 67–90) is simply a restatement of the biblical narrative as found in the Bible. Section 4 (lines 91–134) commences with a plea to Moses to reveal what the true meaning of the narrative and its symbols are. It is from line 99 onwards where the meaning of the ritual finally begins to be deciphered. Jacob begins his interpretation with a display of amazement at the external form of the sacrifice. He claims how the color of the heifer alone suffices to proclaim a slaughtering (99–100). Subsequently, Jacob expresses his amazement at how the sacrifice of the heifer, whose purpose is to purify those who are ritually unclean, renders the officiating priest impure (117–134). He rationalizes that the entire rite must be a symbol of sorts, otherwise this enigma cannot be accounted for. He proceeds to attack the Jewish nation for preferring the symbols of Scripture to the Lord of the symbols. One of the key features of this section is Jacob describing the ritual as being nothing more than a shadow, a term he will use six times in total throughout the homily. For Jacob, the efficacy of the rite rested in the fact that it was a shadow of the Son of God (*bṭelōniteh dbar alōhō*). He plays on a shadow-body analogy and shows himself as being puzzled at how the Jewish people could love the shadow but hate the great body (*gušmō rabō*) casting the shadow – the Lord Himself (109–114).

In section 5 (lines 135–180), Jacob proceeds to question the conundrum of the narrative. He presents a brief, fictional dialogue wherein he asks the priest what the source of his impurity is. When the priest replies that the offering he made was the cause of his own defilement, Jacob logically assumes that if this were the case, then the animal itself would have had to been defiled (135–140). He then proceeds to cast the narrative through the lens of Christian typological exegesis, but not before portraying the cross of Jesus as a key through which the hidden things of Scripture are revealed. Beginning with the color of the animal as itself being an indicator that the rite gestures towards its being a portrayal of Christ's slaughter, Jacob goes on to juxtapose the themes of life and death. He maintains that the reason the heifer was red was so that it would signify both life and death simultaneously: while the animal symbolizes death through its color, yet is it alive and moves towards its death. He interprets the simultaneous presence of life and death in the yet-alive heifer as an image of Christ, in whose death life sprung forth for the world (153–166). Jacob also interprets the color of the animal and its movement towards the place of its slaughter as a symbol of the injured Christ going towards His death (173–178). He summarizes these points well in the final verses of the section: "He poured forth on it a color which proclaimed heavily the death [of the Son], and he proclaimed it a sacrifice that through it he would purify those who are unclean" (179–180).

In section 6 (lines 181–216), Jacob delineates the meaning of the other three materials used in the rite: the hyssop, the scarlet dye, and the cedarwood. According to the homilist, these items were intended to increase the symbolic imagery of the narrative in order to make undisputedly clear that all elements of the rite foreshadowed the crucifixion. As such, the mingling of hyssop, a symbol of purity, with the wool of scarlet dye, another representation of blood, was intended to portray the image of pure blood so as to depict the pure blood of Christ which was shed at the crucifixion (185–188; 195–198). As for the cedarwood, this was included in order to portray the wood of the cross on which the slaughter occurred (189–194). After providing his interpretation on these items and their role in the ritual, Jacob again asks a series of rhetorical questions whose purpose is to confirm the symbolic value of these very elements (211–216).

In section 7 (lines 217–252), Jacob continues interpreting other aspects of the ritual, providing for the audience his most comprehensive assessment of the narrative yet. He begins by describing how the removal of the heifer from the camp to be slaughtered outside is a type of Jesus being crucified outside the city of Jerusalem. Jacob sees the priest going outside the camp with the heifer as a likeness of the Lord who was brought out by the priests to be slayed (233–236). Furthermore, just as the heifer that was slaughtered outside the camp of Israel became a source of sanctification for Israel, so too was Christ's death outside the city walls of Jerusalem a source of sanctification for Israel and the whole world (237–238). Furthermore, Jacob reiterates in this section two typological links already seen earlier in the commentary; the cedarwood brought out of the camp is an image of the cross carried by Jesus to the place of his execution, and the heifer going towards its death while red is a symbol of the Lord going towards His death with His body spotted red with blood from the scourging He had endured (239–242). Finally, Jacob explains the conundrum of the priest becoming defiled from the sacrifice that conveys purity. It is a symbol of the priests who delivered Christ to death and were made impure from the act, even though the sacrifice itself effected purgation for the entire world (243–244). Jacob finishes the section by comparing the water in which the heifer's ashes were mixed in order to be sprinkled, with the water which gushed forth from Jesus' pierced side (245–248). He is able to create this connection on account of the water being a medium of transference for purity in both situations. In the case of the heifer, it is mixed in water for the priest to sprinkle on those suffering from corpse impurity, while for the church, the water flowing from Christ's side is the baptism which purifies and renews the person.[2]

Section 8 (lines 253–286) transitions into Jacob discussing the power of the church's sprinkling and how it is superior to the sprinkling of the heifer's ashes. It is not easy, however, to decipher Jacob's use of the word sprinkling (rsōsō) in the verses here. Whereas in the previous section the ceremonial sprinkling referred to the entirety of Christ's sacrifice, with an emphasis on the blood and water which flowed from His side, here it seems to be alluding to both the overall sacrifice and baptism. This is especially made evident in lines 259–260 and 265–266, where Jacob discusses the restorative properties of this sprinkling. This new sanctification is able to regenerate the individual: the harlot becomes a virgin; the old man becomes a youth. Yet, in lines 261–264, it is referring to biblical figures for whom the act of

---

[2] While Jacob does not explicitly state that the water at the crucifixion is a type for baptism, this is implied on account of the following. First, in stating that the water coming out of Jesus is, alongside the blood, able to purify, he creates a strong typological association between the crucifixion, baptism and the Eucharist, a connection well-attested to in the early Syriac exegetical tradition. Furthermore, in his mimrō on the Partaking of the Holy Mysteries [Homily 95], Jacob makes clear the baptismal dimension of the Eucharist which begins with the piercing of Christ's side on Golgotha (lines 19–44). This close connection between the crucifixion and Christian baptism is seen many times also in Ephrem's poetry. See for example, Hymns on the Nativity 16.10; Hymns on Virginity 15.6, 21.9, 30.10; Nisibene Hymns 39.7; and Hymns on Epiphany 7.1–3. For an overview of this issue, see Sebastian P. Brock, "Baptismal Themes in the writings of Jacob of Serug," in Symposium Syriacum (vol. 205 in Orientalia Christiana Analecta; Rome: Pontificium Institutum Orientalium Studiorum, 1978), 325–47; and Brock "Some Important Baptismal Themes in the Syriac Tradition," Harp 4 (1991): 189–214. For Jacob's homily on the Holy Mysteries, see Amir Harrak, trans., Jacob of Sarug's Homily on the Partaking of the Holy Mysteries (vol. 19 of Texts from Christian Late Antiquity; ed. George A. Kiraz; Piscataway: Gorgias Press, 2013).

baptism was not applicable. The context of these verses would indicate that the sprinkling also refers to the grace of the overall redemptive act of the crucifixion. Further on, Jacob interprets the priest sprinkling blood seven times towards the Tabernacle as an instruction to the people to guard the seven gates of their soul (280).[3] He, of course, instructs that this guarding can only be accomplished through the cross, by acquiring God's color in the soul, and kindling one's soul towards God (283–286). Thus, the cedarwood, the scarlet dye and the fire of the offering are symbols of what one requires to safeguard the soul from the dangers of the stranger (*nukrōyō*) seeking to enter therein.

In section 9 (lines 287–318), Jacob merges the mystery of the Eucharist into this concept of the church's sprinkling. He presents a typological association between the great fire in which the heifer is entirely consumed and the Eucharistic bread. Within three stanzas, Jacob successfully creates such a connection by comparing the purifying properties of fire with that of the bread of the Son (295–298; 301–302). He conceives the Eucharistic bread as being infused with a cathartic fire that purifies

---

[3] It is difficult to know from where Jacob inherited the idea of the soul having seven gates, as no other patristic authority, Syriac or otherwise, mentions this. While there is a symbolic use of the number seven throughout the scriptures (see for example Isaiah 11:1–3, Zechariah 3:9, 4:10, and Revelations 1:4; 3:1; 4:5; 5:6), at no point is it used to refer to the senses or the gates of the soul. There is, however, the possibility that Jacob may in fact be transmitting here a tradition found circulating in Jewish mystical circles during his time. *Sefer Yetzirah*, the oldest of kabbalistic texts believed by most scholars to have been compiled between the second and sixth centuries CE, contains such a teaching. The anonymous author believes that God took the seven letters of the Hebrew Bible that take a *dagesh* (BGD KPRT) and therefore had two modes of pronunciation, and molded from their special nature the seven planets of the universe, the seven days in the week, and the seven gates of the soul: two eyes, two ears, two nostrils and the mouth. See *Sefer Yetzirah* 4:6–14 in Aryeh Kaplan, *Sefer Yetzirah: The Book of Creation* (Rev. ed.; Boston: Weiser Books, 1997), 167–184.

the individual receiving it. These ideas resonate strongly with those seen in some of Ephrem's works, most notably in several of his hymns.[4] Furthermore, Jacob equates the purified site on which the heifer is slaughtered and burnt with the church wherein the bread of the Lord is distributed affectionately towards all her children (300–301). Again, as seen in earlier sections, he compares the strength of the shadow with that of the antitype, the very substance of the Lord (305–306). He finishes by comparing the old purification rite with the new. Jacob claims the current process for being renewed is superior to the old as there is no longer a need for any of the old prescriptions. The cross alone suffices to purify and give life as it is both the embodiment and the summation of all the old sacrifices (307–318).

Section 10 (lines 319–344) continues in the theme established at the end of the previous section. Jacob continues to emphasize how the church no longer requires the animals of the past in order to purify someone. Bulls and heifers are useless as it is the blood of Christ and the cross which make whole the individual. He makes a powerful statement when he claims that God does not desire any material object but rather the person's being alone (323–324). In the last section, Jacob goes into an anti-Jewish rhetoric wherein he asks the Jewish people to cease serving the shadows of the past and to accept enlightenment through the cross. He tells them that they are defiled on account of having sacrificed Christ but that they can become purified on

---

[4] See hymns 10 and 19 from Ephrem's *Hymns on Faith* cycle in Jeffrey T. Wickes, trans. *St. Ephrem the Syrian: The Hymns on Faith* (vol. 130 of *The Fathers of the Church: A New Translation*; ed. David G. Hunter et al.; Washington: The Catholic University of America Press, 2015), 121–5, 151–3. For a discussion of fire imagery in connection with offerings, the Holy Spirit, and the Eucharist, see Sebastian P. Brock, "Fire from Heaven: from Abel's Sacrifice to the Eucharist," in *Fire from Heaven: Studies in Syriac Theology and Liturgy* (vol. 863 of *Variorum Collected Studies Series*; London: Ashgate Variorum, 2006), 229–243.

account of this same sacrifice (325–340).[5] He finishes the section by claiming how accepting Christ does not mean that one abolishes the law (341–342).

In summary, this homily is an exegetical piece, typical of the patristic age, which situates a rite described in the Hebrew Bible within a Christian type-antitype interpretive framework. Jacob's objective is to juxtapose the symbols with what he perceives to be their respective realities, in order to show that the complex and enigmatic red heifer rite can be easily understood in light of Christ's passion and death. Staying true to patristic typology, Jacob's objective is to display for his audience the weak and temporary efficacy of the symbol in the old ritual against the enduring and permanent strength of Christ's sacrifice in the New Testament. Indeed, the ashes of the heifer had the ability to purify, but the purity it bestowed on its recipient was temporary since encountering another corpse or grave would return the individual back into a state of impurity, requiring the purification-process to be repeated. But Christ's sacrifice, according to Jacob, brings about a permanent state of purity for those willing to be sprinkled by his blood, since it is the summation of all offerings prescribed in the Old Covenant. Being the epitome of all past biblical sacrifices, Christ's offering has the ability to purify indefinitely not only corpse impurity, but all

---

[5] The statements of Jacob in this section resonate strongly with the remarks of Aphrahat in his fourth Demonstration. Aphrahat states that the Jews have been stained red on account of the blood of Christ and of the prophets, and can be cleansed only through baptism and their participation in the Eucharist. He also stresses that the sacrifices of old are rejected and God now requires a spiritual offering – prayer. He writes, "Blood is atoned for by the Blood, and body is purified by the Body. Sins are washed away in water, and prayer speaks with [God's] majesty. Observe, my friend, that sacrifices and offerings have been rejected, and that prayer has been chosen instead." Adam Lehto, *The Demonstrations of Aphrahat, the Persian Sage* (Vol. 27 of *Gorgias Eastern Christian Studies*; ed. George A. Kiraz et al.; Piscataway: Gorgias Press, 2010), 4:19 (144–5).

forms of defilement, and to wholly renew the individual. For Jacob, the heifer possessed power to purify, not on account of some innate property it contained. Rather, the purgative properties of its ashes rested solely in the symbol which was portrayed by the rite. The ashes were able to cleanse only because the animal's ritualistic slaughter was a type of the slaying which would purify the world – the crucifixion. Thus, through the power of the cross, operating by means of the heifer and the other prescribed animals, was sanctification possible in the Old Testament.

Jacob is certainly not the first church writer to comment on the red heifer ritual. The late first/early second century CE *Epistle of Barnabas* is the earliest document to append a Christological interpretation to the rite.[6] While the treatment of the topic in this piece is quite brief, it does establish the ritual as a type of the crucifixion. Later patristic authorities to also deal with this narrative in more detail include Epiphanius of Salamis, Theodoret of Cyrus and Cyril of Alexandria, the latter two of which portray the ritual as a prefigurement of Christ's death and the purification that this sacrifice brought about for the entire world.[7] Given the number of times Cyril of Alexandria deals with the matter, his consistent typological application of Christ's passion and death to the various components of the narrative, as well as the fact that he was an author whom both the Chalcedonians and Anti-Chalcedonians respected and utilized, it is possible to surmise that he served as the inspiration for Jacob's

---

[6] Barnabas, *Epistola Catholica VIII* (PG 2:748A-749A).

[7] Epiphanius, *Panarion* (PG 41:457C-460B); Cyril of Alexandria, *Glaphyrorum in Numeros Liber* (PG 69:623B-636C); Cyril of Alexandria, *Commentarius in Oseam Prophetam* (PG 71:125A-B); Cyril of Alexandria, *Commentarius in Malachiam Prophetam* (PG 72:309A-B); Cyril of Alexandria, *Collectanea: Ex Libro Numerorum* (PG 77:1225A-1232B); Theodoret, *Quaestiones in Numeros XIX: Interrogatio XXXV & XXXVI* (PG 80:385A-388A); Theodoret, *Interpretatio Epistolae ad Hebraeos XIII* (PG 82:781C-D); Theodoret, *Eranistes Seu Polymorphus: Impatibilis, Dialogus III* (PG 83:253A-B);

treatment of the topic. However, there are marked differences between the two authors. Aside the obvious difference that Cyril writes in prose while Jacob writes in verse, Jacob examines Numbers 19 to a degree not seen in either Cyril or any of the other church author. His verbose and detailed treatment of the story is such that makes it the preeminent commentary of the ritual throughout the entire patristic world.

In closing, I would like to mention the following. First, I am indebted to Amir Harrak, Professor of Aramaic and Syriac studies at the University of Toronto, for his invaluable insights on this difficult text and for his suggestions on my translation. Second, it is important to mention that an English translation of this *mimrō* was already made many years ago by David J. Lane (1935–2005), former Associate Professor of Near Eastern Studies at the University of Toronto.[8] I am especially honored to have obtained my Ph.D. at the very school and department which once housed this extraordinary scholar, and which continues to be one of the few places worldwide wherein one can study the Syriac language and culture. It is hoped that the introduction and translation presented in this fascicle, both made independently of any and all previous scholarship on the matter, will generate or renew interest in the patristic, typological-interpretive approach applied to this obscure and perplexing biblical ritual by one of the greatest poet-exegetes of the Eastern Church – Mar Jacob.

SUMMARY

1. Opening Invocation (1–36)

2. Moses' Writings Filled with Symbols of the Son of God (37–66)

3. Numbers 19 – The Red Heifer Ritual (67–90)

---

[8] David J. Lane, "Jacob of Sarug: On the Red Heifer," *Harp* 15 (2002): 25–42.

TEXT AND TRANSLATION

MEMRA 77:

CONCERNING THE RED HEIFER WHICH IS COMMANDED IN THE LAW TO BE BURNT IN PLACE OF THE SINS OF THE ASSEMBLY[1]: AND CONCERNING THE CRUCIFIXION OF OUR LORD

1   Behold, I approach the treasury of Your mysteries to make trade
        [with it].
    Grant me an abundance from the wealth of Your crucifixion!
    My mind conceives the suffering of Your death, O Son of God.
    Through the pangs of Your slaughter, may it beget the discourse
        of truth.[2]
5   Your blood moves greatly in me; I shall mingle the wine of Your
        sacrifice.
    Pour it in me and I will irrigate the thirsty nations from Your
        fount!
    Mingle Your new and divine wine without sparing,
    for while they are guarding it and are being guarded by it, they
        will be entrusted to You.
    Grant me a word, not that I am going to contain Your hidden-
        ness,
10 but that I may speak in wonder, for You are unfathomable.
    The waves of Your discourses kick me violently as I bathe within
        the raging seas.
    Grant me your hand, O Lord of the seas, that I may be drawn
        out by it!
    Your mysteries surround me like legions of all sorts of warriors,
    and each one pulled me to speak to me concerning Your revela-
        tions.

---

[1] [Editor's note]: Numbers 19:1–10
[2] London [L]: ܫܪܪܟ, "your truth."

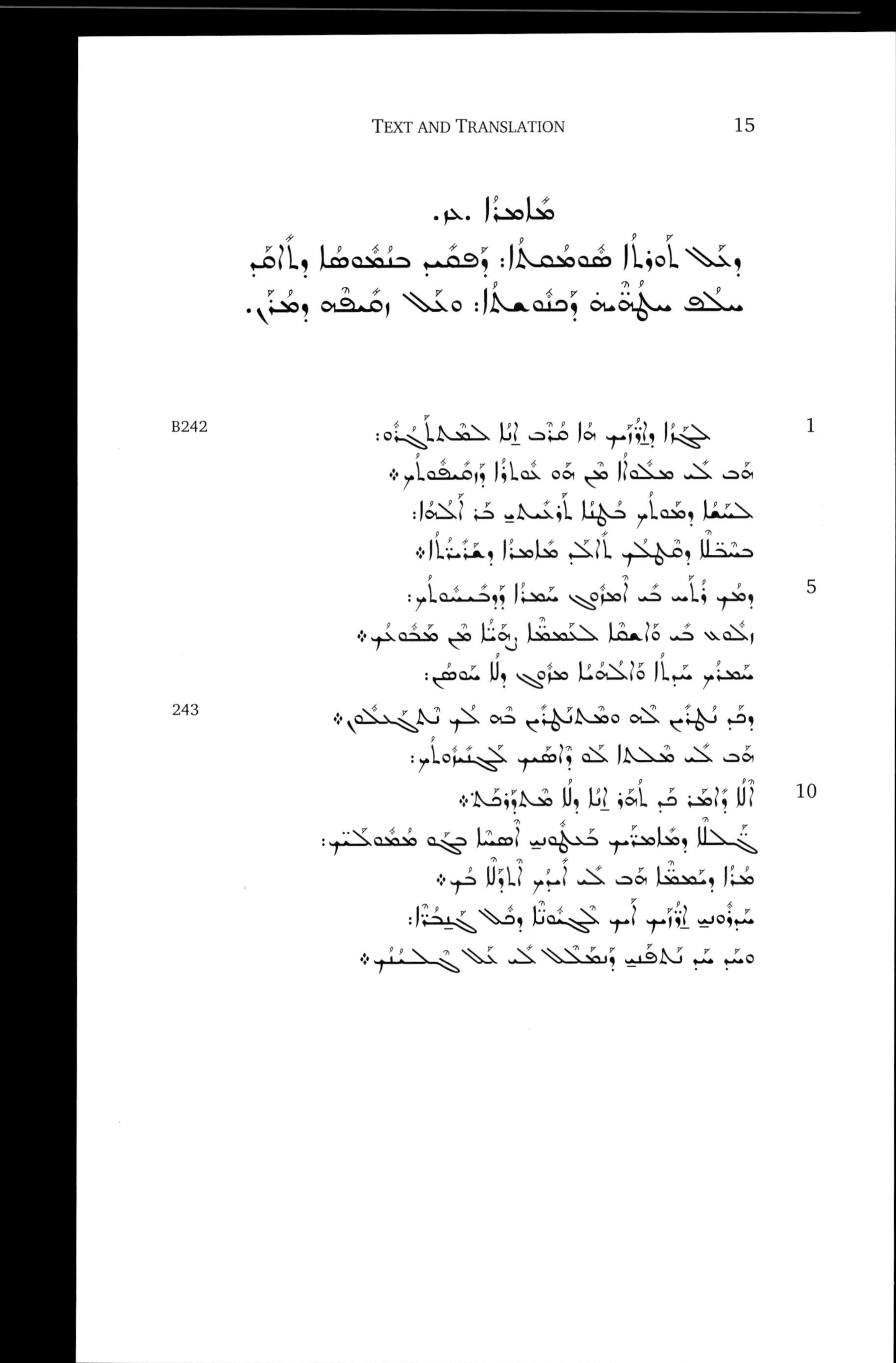

15   I saw the wealth of symbols which were heaped up on the road
          of the books,
      and the task fell on me to carry from it and to flourish exceed-
          ingly by it.
      The instruction concerning the banquet[3] of Your great slaughter
          called me
      and it mingled blood for me, and lo, it boils in me to show its
          power.
      Moses, who was able, made a spiritual banquet.
20   And he set the table of symbols before me that I may be
          delighted by it.
      The books of the Father I took to read out, and from them I
          learned
      that He has a Son, and look, He is spoken of between their vers-
          es!
      The mystery of Your slaughter was transmitted in their revela-
          tions,
      and the image of Your death[4] was portrayed in a suffering[5] upon
          their scrolls.
25   There is not as much water in the great sea
      as the book of Moses which is filled with the symbols of our
          Lord.
      The sky is not illumined by the moon which travels in it,
      as much as the Pentateuch that shines out with the story of the
          Son of God.
      The sun is not as adorned by the rays which surround it

---

[3] Oxford [O]: ܢܠܘܬܐ "banquets."

[4] Sic O: ܛܘܦܣܝ, "Your type."

[5] L: ܘܪܒܬܐ ܨܘܪܬܟ ܪܒ ܗܘܐ ܡܢ ܪܫ ܥܠ ܡܓܠܬܗܘܢ "And Your great image was portrayed from the beginning upon their scrolls."

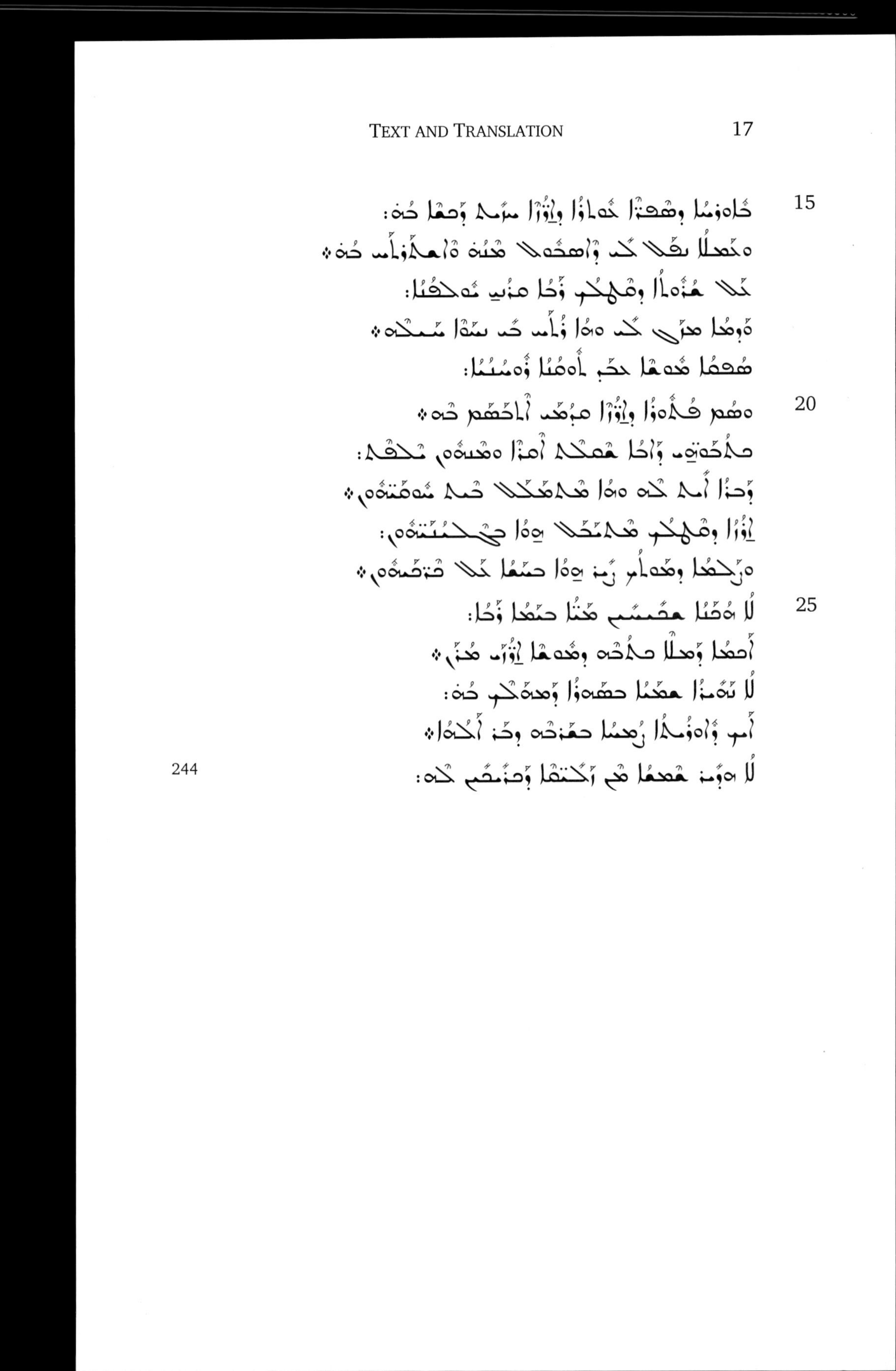

30   as the book of the Father which shows the beauty[6] of the Son.
    The heat is not as near to the flame
    as the cross is clearly portrayed in the scriptures.
    All who prophesied concerning the hidden things [of scripture]
        spoke through our Lord.
    And unless it is [so], the revelations of truth would be futile.
35   The scriptures are for Him limbs as He is the soul for them.
    And through Him, they are moved to speak [of] Him richly.
    Moses carried[7] the choice colors of prophecy
    and depicted Him on all the leaves through his readings.
    With the blood of the sacrifices, he sprinkles[8] the road of the
        crucifixion,
40   so as to honor the great slaughter which proceeds on it.
    He shed blood against iniquity when it had been intensified,
    and he mystically made atonement for the nation through its
        sacrifices.
    The cross of our Lord[9] was foretold of in his works,
    and there is nothing which he did[10] without it.
45   In all sorts of ways, he [Moses] celebrated the symbol of the Son
        of God,
    so that with all kinds of beauty he might establish for Him an
        image that is entirely astonishing.
    The heifer he sacrificed for the cleansing of all the people,
    that it would be sprinkled on whomsoever had sinned, and they
        were made pure.[11]
    If there is a hearing ear which receives me in a loving way,

---

[6] L: ܣܘܢܐ "the story."

[7] L: ܫܩܝܠ "is carrying."

[8] L: ܕܡܐ ܕܕܒܚܐ ܪܫ ܠܐܘܪܚܐ ܕܩܝܣܐ ܪܫܘܡܗ "With the blood of the sacrifice he draws up the road of the crucifixion."

[9] L: ܕܒܪܐ "of the Son."

[10] L: ܘܥܒܕ

[11] L: ܘܢܬܕܟܘܢ ܒܗ "that they may be made pure by it."

أمِر 30

لا :

أمِر

 أمِر : 35

50   then the mystery of the narrative I have taken up to tell is
            wondrous.
        But if love is not present in the listening,
        the symbols of Moses will not be depicted clearly.
        If your entire mind is in the world [and] is intent on acquisi-
            tion,[12]
        you will not be able to hear from my mouth the story which I
            will undertake.
55   If ephemeral affairs are dear to you,
        it is difficult for Scripture[13] to speak to you concerning the hid-
            den things.
        But unless your soul inclines towards God in love,
        Moses utters empty sounds to your ear.
        Moses is a stammerer[14] and does not expound to you whatsoever
            he says.
60   Send your mind to enter [the book of Moses] and understand his
            hidden things![15]
        If his distinctive features do not abound,
        [then] read in love, and lo, he establishes you over his revela-
            tions!
        His discourse is not easy; if you look carefully [he only gives]
            hints.
        He depicts the cross – fix your mind to its deeds.
65   It is not possible to purify anything except through blood,
        and there is neither life nor atonement except through our Lord.
        Give[16] heed to me that I may speak now being amazed,
        concerning that red heifer which had been slain.
        Why does the priest cast it out from the people?

---

[12] O: ܠܒܪ ܐܝܟ ܡܢ ... :ܩܢܝܢܐ "possessions: ... to hear from us."

[13] L: ܟܬܒܝ "my book."

[14] O: ܥܓܠܐ "the calf." See Exodus 4:10.

[15] O: ܟܣܝܬܐ "the hidden things."

[16] L: ܗܒܘ

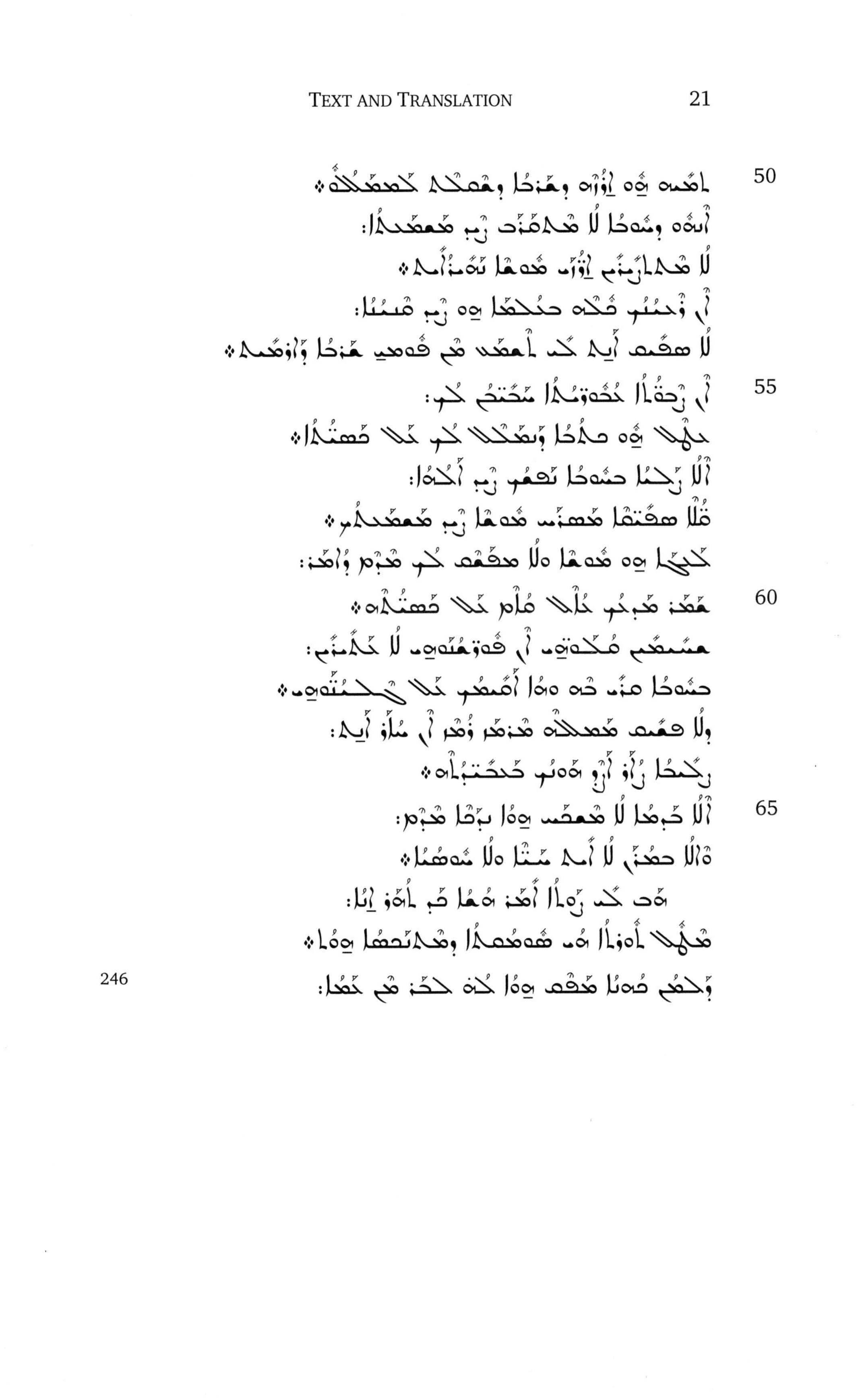

70   And by what symbol did he burn it? And for what [reason]?
    Let Scripture come and explain itself in simple terms,
    then the interpretation will display the beauty of the lesson. [17]
    The Lord said to Moses and to Aaron concerning the people,
    by what [manner] and how it could be purified when it had be-
        come defiled.
75   "Choose a red heifer which is pure and without blemish,
    and upon which no yoke had been placed to subjugate from its
        [early] days. [18]
    And give it to the priest Eleazar when it is required,
    and the priest will bring it out of the encampment and will slay
        it there.
    And he will take of the blood and will sprinkle it towards the
        front of the Tabernacle.
80   And he will burn it in fire, [along with] its skin and flesh and
        blood.
    And its dung [will also be burnt] along with it. And the priest
        will take cedarwood,
    and he will bring with him hyssop, and scarlet dye.
    And he will cast [these] into the fire, into the conflagration of
        the red heifer which he brought [for an offering].
    And the priest will wash his garments and will bathe his flesh in
        water.
85   And after these things he will enter the encampment,
    and the priest will also be unclean until evening.
    And whoever burnt it will wash his clothing and bathe his flesh.
    And this one will also be unclean until evening.
    And a man who is clean will gather the ashes of that burning,

---

[17] L: ܡܐܪ "the lessons."

[18] Stanzas 38–45 are a recitation of Numbers 19:2–9 which describe the ceremony of the red heifer.

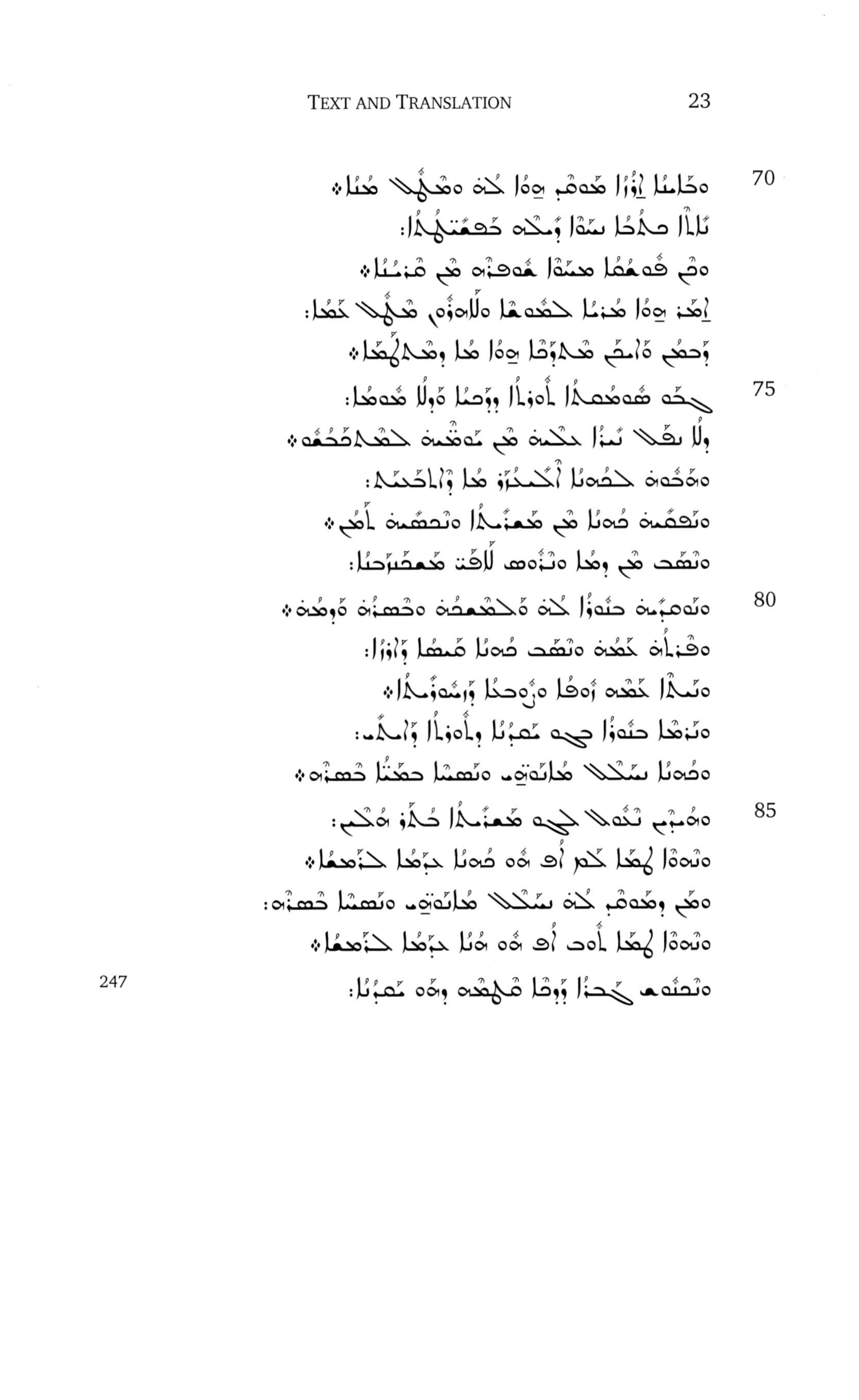

90   that it may be for the sprinkling of the entire assembly, that it
      would become purified on account of it."
      O Moses! What is this that you are saying?
      The symbols that were pronounced by you, O Great Prophet, are
          astonishing!
      Exalted in the manner of revelations, proffer to us a word so
          that we may see its beauty.
      O bearer of parables, raise the veil from your narrative!
95   You who were raised up to the lofty utterance of the House of
          God,
      come down! Tell us of the symbols which you brought from the
          heights!
      You who penetrated and saw the Son with His Begetter,
      come out! Show us clearly and openly about his beauty!
      The form of this sacrifice which you presented is amazing.
100   For even while it was not [yet] slaughtered, the color of blood is
          shown in it.
      But if – just as you say – the heifer was needed for the sacrifice,
      why [was it] red unless its color proclaimed a slaughtering?
      But if the unclean ones are purified by your sacrifice, O Moses,
      why did the priest who slaughtered it become impure, unless it
          be a symbol?
105   O truth which is revealed and stands as a luminary,
      but the blind nation does not see that it was entirely light.
      The symbols of our Lord used to cleanse it from impurity,
      but now that the Lord of the symbols has come, why do they
          hate Him?
      By the shadow of the Son of God, it [the Jewish Nation] was
          purified,

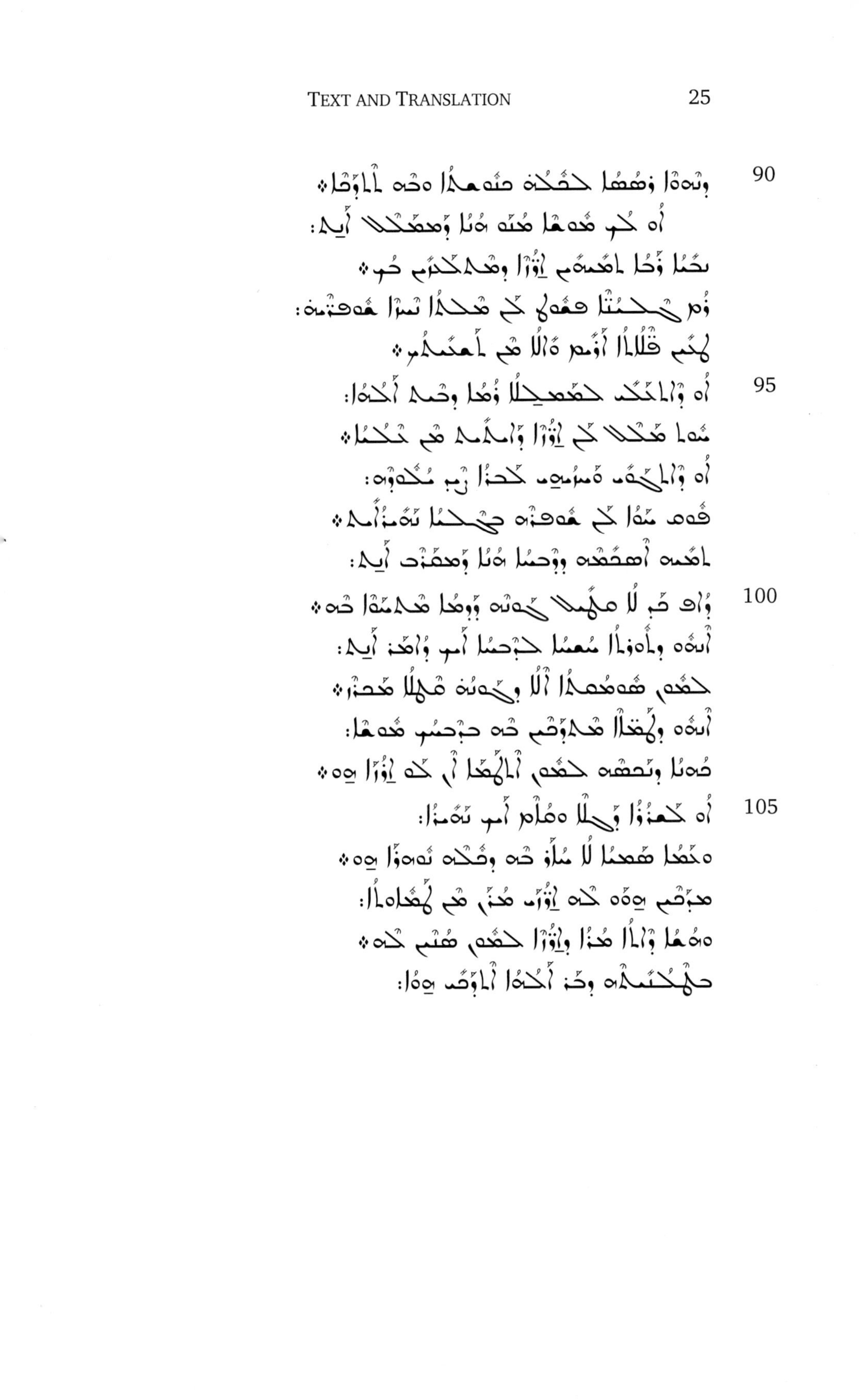

110   but today, when the Great Body has appeared, it does not love
           Him!
       It attached itself to various sorts of borrowed sacrifices.
       But look! The Lord of Truth is placed before it yet it does not
           look at Him.
       The blind nation took hold of the shadow and abandoned the
           body.
       And, furthermore, it did not recognize that the body[19] is also the
           Savior.
115   It did not understand that Moses had made it pure through the
           parables,
       and [that] he depicted something [more] by these symbols
           which he was presenting.
       Why did the pure sacrifice make the one offering it unclean,
       except to depict a type of our Lord and His crucifiers?
       The nation suspended our Lord on wood and it became impure,
120   but the blood of His sprinkling purified the nations and
           sanctified them.
       For those who slaughtered Him became impure but they who
           consume Him found life.
       That those who killed Him died through Him but those who eat
           [Him] find life, is a great marvel!
       The priest who slaughtered the heifer became defiled according
           to the Law,
       that he would become the likeness of the nation which boldly
           crucified [Him].

---

[19] L: ‎‎ܠܡܫܐ "In the sensation [of the handling]."

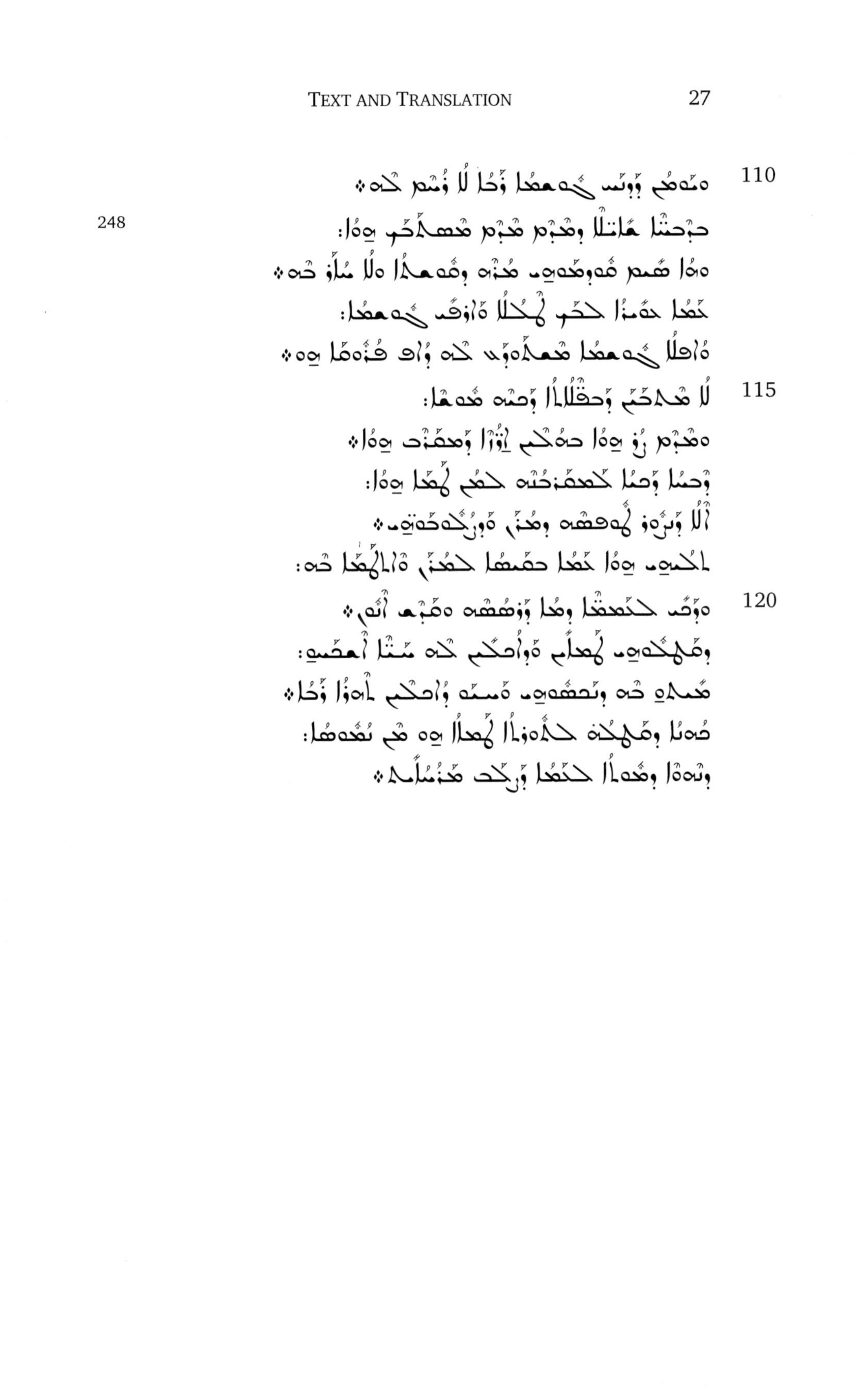

125   And if this which I have spoken is not[20] truthful,
    why did the priest become defiled by the sacrifice which he
        brought?
    He [the priest] purified these ones [Israelites], but he[21] became
        unclean symbolically.
    Others gained but he suffered loss in the sacrifice which he
        made.
    When the priest brought the heifer out from the nation
130   he made it a sacrifice, [yet] he became defiled[22] by the sacrifice
        which he made.
    His action[23] is good in that he purified those who are unclean.
    As for him, the sacrifice which he offered made him unclean.
    The priest remained within the encampment while being un-
        clean,
    and they fled from him till evening for he was defiled.[24]
135   Tell me, O priest, that impurity – because of what is it?
    O priest of the nation, what made you unclean while you were
        pure?
    The priest says, "The sacrifice defiled me when I offered it,
    And my offering is the entire reason for my becoming impure."
    O priest of the nation, the sacrifice which you brought was then
        unclean.

---

[20] O: ܠܐ
[21] O: ܘܠܗܘ "but that one."
[22] O: ܐܬܛܡܐ
[23] O: ܢܚܒܗ "He did [a good]."
[24] L: ܗܘܐ

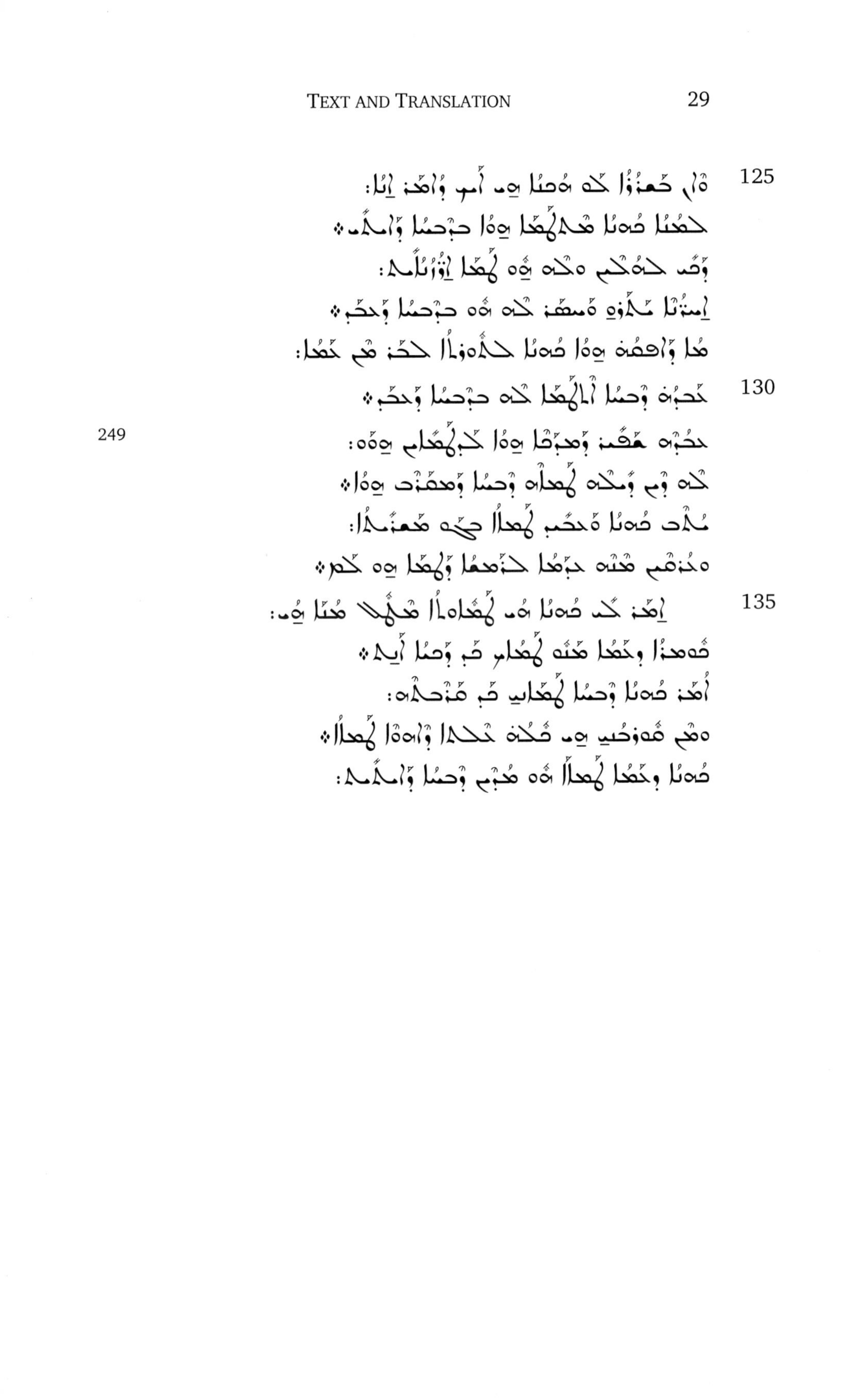

249

140   Why did you offer it if impurity was found in it?
      So then, your likeness is entirely depicted[25] in the children of
           your nation,
      and your whole sacrifice proclaims our Lord who purifies all.
      Look! Through the cross, all is truly purified![26]
      The nation alone became defiled by it[27] for it did not love it.
145   The symbols which Moses the scribe depicted in his writings are
           marvellous.
      And if not through our Lord, their actions would not be deci-
           phered.
      He buried treasures concealing them amongst his verses,
      but the cross came [and] revealed his hidden things.
      If you are discerning,[28] concentrate your mind on his actions
150   and you will find that in every instance, he depicted for us the
           Son.
      He depicted a great image of our Lord when he sacrificed;
      the symbolic heifer put on the color of the crucifixion.
      It was red so that its appearance, too, would proclaim death,
      so as to resemble the sprinkled blood while yet alive.

---

[25] O: ܙܢܝܟ ܗܘ ܘܟܠܗ ܨܝܪ – the words are the same but are arranged differently.

[26] O: ܡܬܚܒܠ "was injured."

[27] O: ܠܗ "to it."

[28] L: ܦܪܘܫ

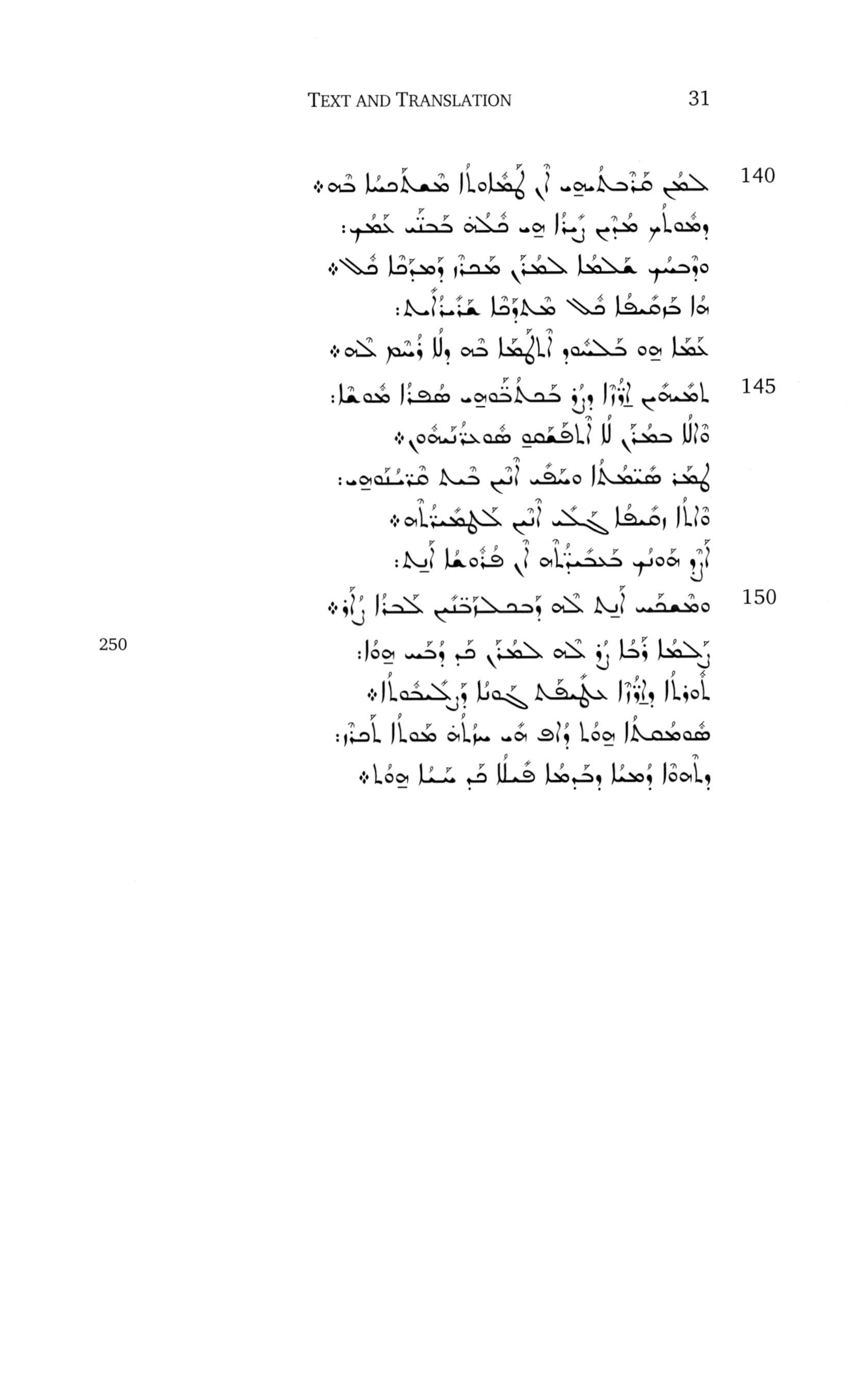

155   The symbol colored the whole sacrifice with the color of
        suffering,
    so that its likeness would hint at slaughter to the one looking at
        it.
    While not [yet] slain, the appearance of the heifer which he
        brought was perfect.[29]
    It was like blood for its color was red.
    When he chose it, he adorned the symbol in the color of slaugh-
        ter,
160   so that the crucifixion would be clearly shown in it.
    Like a mirror of blood, he set it up that they would see it
    and see death which was moving symbolically in it.
    It was slain in color but living through the symbol which was
        spoken of through it –
    clearly the story of the slaughter of the One who gives life to all.
165   It was colored in slaughter and was moving while alive toward
        death,
    like that sacrifice of the Son out of whose death life sprang
        forth.
    And if this is not just as I have said,
    why was a red heifer chosen to be sacrificed?
    He saw in it the color of the crucifixion when he chose it,
170   and he gave it for a burnt-offering that it would be sprinkled on
        the entire nation.
    The blood was depicted through it and it proclaimed openly the
        death of the Son,
    who became for the nations a sprinkling that purifies all impuri-
        ty.
    Its body bore the sprinkling of the scourges and then was cho-
        sen,
    so that the sentence of the slaughter might be spoken richly
        through it.

---

[29] L: ܒ ܠܐ ܡܝܬ ܗ ܚܙܬܐ ܕܥܓܠܬܐ ܕܗܘ ܐܝܬܝ ܗܘܬ ܐܒܝܠܬܐ, "While not [yet] slain, the appearance of the heifer which he brought was mournful."

155

160

165

170

251

175 He depicted the wounds upon it in appearance while it was not
         yet beaten,
     that through its color it would proclaim the wounds of the Son.
     He adorned it in scourges while it was distant from scourges,
     that by this also it would proclaim the flagellation of the Son.
     He poured forth[30] on it a color which proclaimed heavily the
         death [of the Son],
180 and he proclaimed it a sacrifice that through it he would purify
         those who are unclean.
     Furthermore, he mingled hyssop and scarlet dye with it,
     to make a double[31] symbol of the type of the complete slaughter.
     In all forms, the skillful Moses portrayed blood,
     that in all sorts of colors he would establish the image of the
         crucifixion.
185 The heifer which he brought, that was red, did not suffice for
         him,
     but through the scarlet dye he depicted the blood.
     He mingled wisely the color of blood in one another,
     that the beauty of the image of the crucifixion would become
         strong.
     Why did he take with him the cedarwood?
190 Look O discerning one! The symbol portrays the entire sacrifice!
     He devised the cross but without the wood it cannot stand up.
     But the work of the crucifixion was fulfilled in all things.
     On account of this Moses took the cedarwood,[32]
     that the cross of our Lord would be fulfilled in his actions.

---

[30] L: ܣܟܝ, "He poured out."
[31] O: ܕܢܟܣܘܬ; L: ܢܟܣܘܬ, "to make modest."
[32] O: ܐܪܙܢܝ, "the symbolic [wood]"

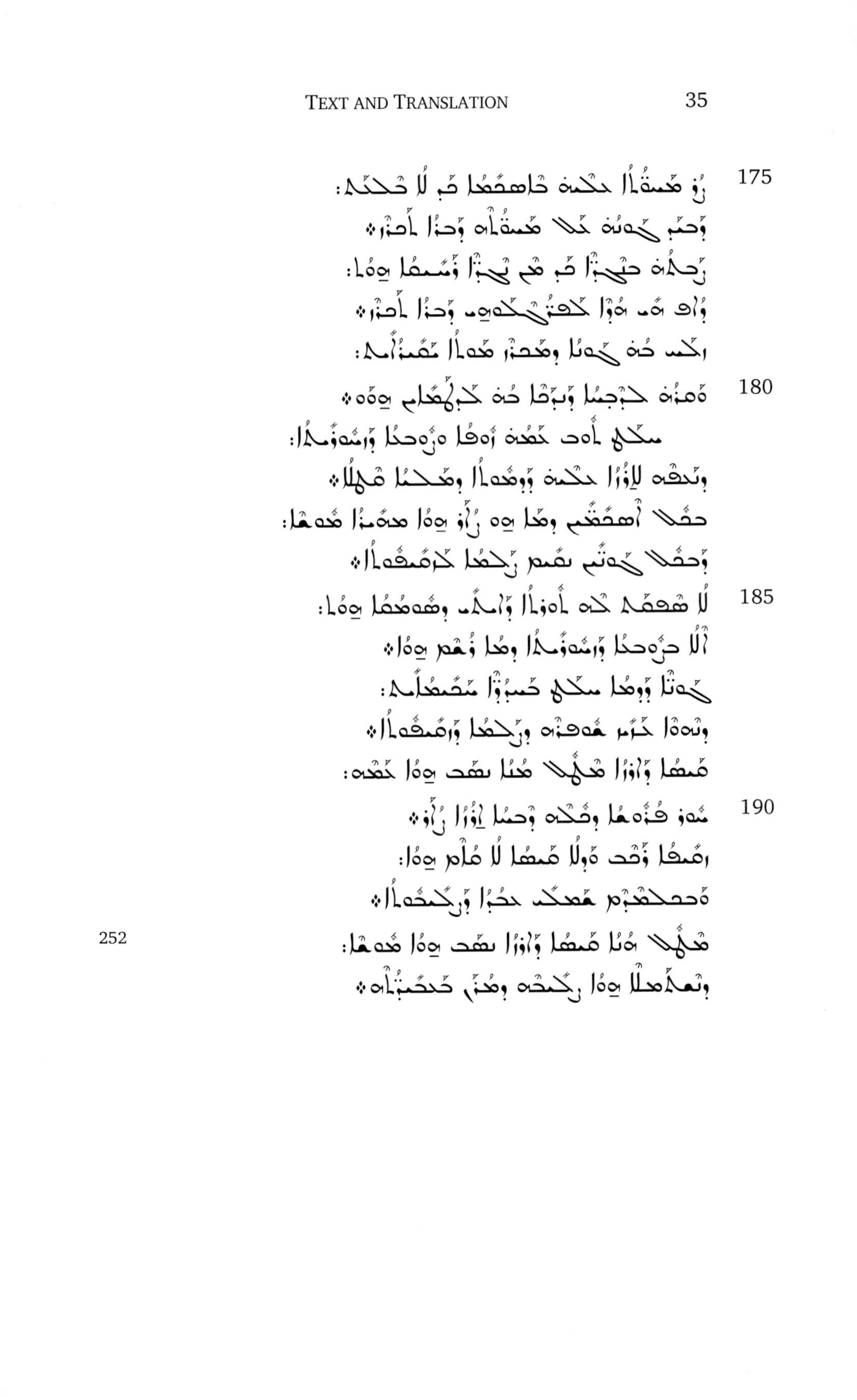

195   He prepared with scarlet dye the sacrifice that he made,
     that the pure blood would be spoken of in his work.
     Through the sprinkled hyssop[33] and the scarlet, the blood was
         portrayed,
     and through the heifer, whose color[34] was red, the entire slaugh-
         ter.[35]
     A deaf person recognizes these symbols through a nod,
200   and a blind person perceives through touch[36] their meanings.[37]
     The nation was more blind than a blind one who does not per-
         ceive.
     Its eyes were opened but its mind was darkened from under-
         standing.[38]
     If it desired to concentrate on these symbols,
     it would see – without stumbling – the cross of the Son in them.
205   From the visible things it would be able to understand the
         hidden things,
     and through the visible things it would understand the con-
         cealed things.
     From the form[39] of these sacrifices which it offered,
     it would understand that a great slaughter saves the world.
     It was easy for it to understand through the types that it was
         serving,

---

[33] O: ܙܘܦܐ – missing the prepositional ܒ.

[34] O: ܕܕܡܗ, "whose blood."

[35] O: ܟܠܗ

[36] The entire first part of this line is omitted in O. Only the very last word, ܦܘܪܫܢܝܗܘܢ, is present.

[37] See Isaiah 35:5.

[38] L: ܘܐܬܦܬܚ ܥܝܢܝܗ ܘܚܫܟ ܠܒܗ ܡܢ ܣܘܟܠܐ "Its eyes were opened but its heart was darkened from understanding." See Isaiah 43:8; John 12:38–40; Matthew 23:16–22.

[39] L: ܐܣܟܡܐ "forms."

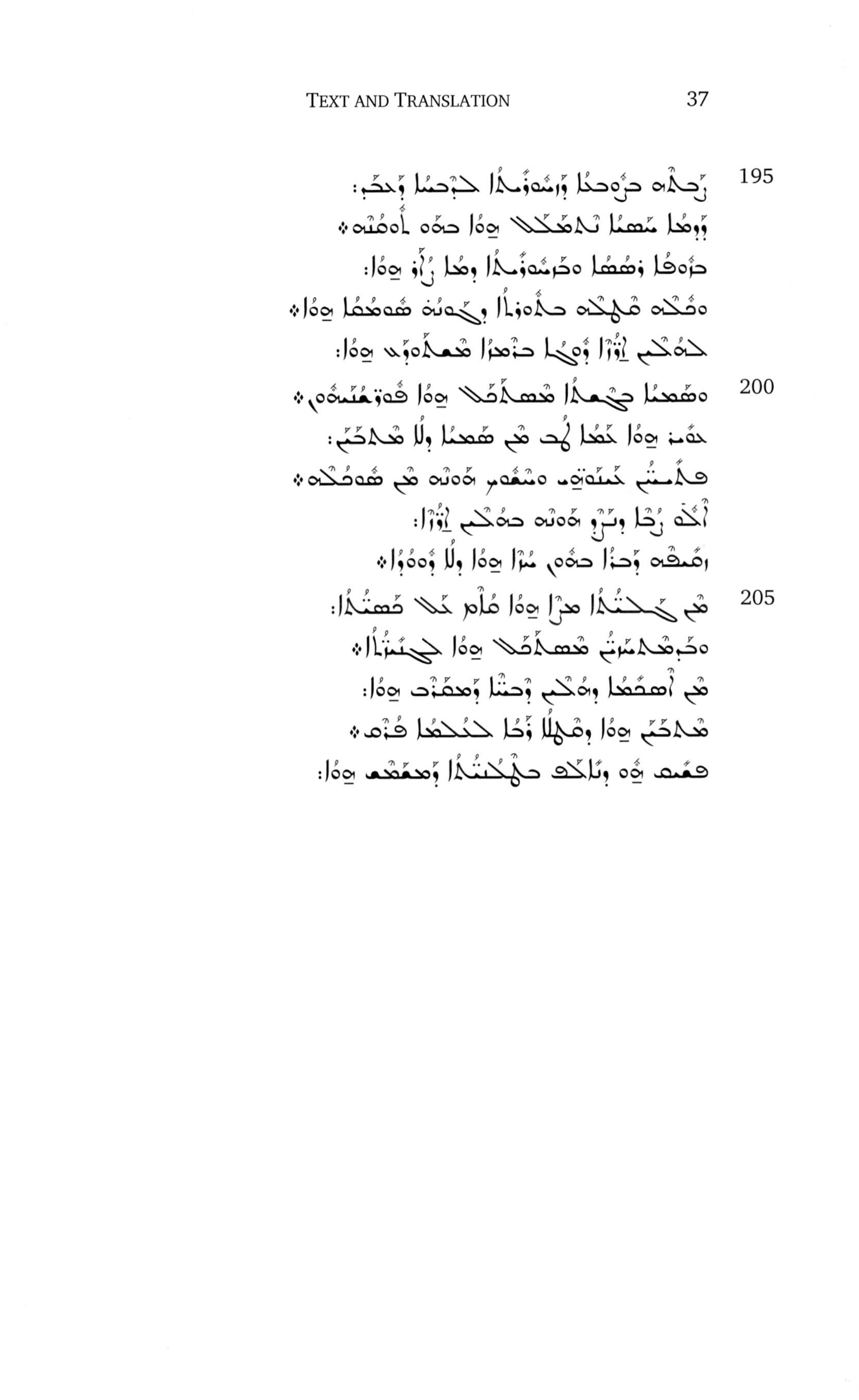

210 for something great was going on within them.
What profit [is there] in the small wool of scarlet?
And by what power did it cleanse from impurity?
What did the cedarwood profit the one who was defiled?
For with it, the Law instructed that the entire nation should be
    purified.
215 Why did he choose the heifer which was red[40] for the sacrifice?
And why were the defiled ones of the nation made pure through
    it?
Something else was spoken of through these sacrifices,[41]
but the nation did not understand that it should know mystical
    things.
Moses hinted to it the slaughter of the Son that saved the world.
220 But because it was blind from understanding, it did not
    perceive.
If that which purified from defilement was a heifer,
why did Moses not choose a black one for the sacrifice?
If he had not been prefiguring the color of the crucifixion,
a red one would not have been required to be the sacrifice.
225 He was proclaiming the blood through the wool and the scarlet
    dye,
that the color of the slaughter will purify the nation from de-
    filement.
Through the shadow of our Lord, Moses purified the nation;
for sheep and oxen did not purify it from defilement.
Look! Through something which was feeble, he is showing it[42]
    something great!

---

[40] L: ‏ܣܘܡܩܬܐ‎

[41] L: ‏ܒܗ ܕܕܒܚܐ‎ "through the sacrifice."

[42] L: ‏ܚܘܝ ܗܘܐ‎

210 وَلِيحِه مُسمَّى مُبْرَم وُجُا مُحَمَّحَى يِوهُا.

حَيَعِزُا رِجُوزُا وَرِشَوَزُىكُا مَى شَءاوُنُا:

وجَامُنا مَسِلا حبِّجْا بِوهُا مَد مَى لَمُجُاوءاُا.

253

مَممُا وَاوزُا مَى مَهِنا بِوهُا جربِمَحلَمُعَا:

وجُه نُمُوهُا هصَر ﻧﻜﻭُّجَا مُحْده جَمُا.

215 ﻟﻜﻭﺯﻟُﺍ حبِّحمْا حصَى حِجُا بِوهُا وِهُومُحُا بِوهُا:

وهُنيْهُلا هُنا لَهُخُاُا وجَمُا حُه مُحْاوَّجُمِ.

اسِزُنا مُبْرَم مُحَمَّحَكَلا بِوهُا حهُكُم وِّحِنَا:

وَلا اُهِجُّحَكَلا جَمُا وتِّر وُومِسُاَكُمِ.

وهُمِ حُه مُومْا وهُجِحُه وَجُا حِنُحِعْا هُنِّم:

220 وهَكَلا وَحمَمِنِ بِوهُا مَى حُومُنا لُا اُهِجُّحَكَلا.

اُ لَمُوزُا بِوهُا اهُ هُمِ وَهبِّحمْا مَى لَمُجُاوءاُا:

حصَى اُومُحمّا لُا لِحُجُا بِوهُا حبِّحمْا مُومْا.

اُنُّه حِيُّومُه وَرِكُمحُواُا لُا محنِّر بِوهُا:

كُه مُومُحممُا مُحَمَّحمْا بِوهُا لَمُوزُا وِّحمْا.

225 حَيَعِزُا ورُوحُا وَرِشَوَزُىكُا ومُا مُحمّر بِوهُا:

وحِيُّومُه وهُجِلِلا بِرِّجُا حجَمُا مَى لَمُجُاوءاُا.

حهُحُكُنِيُكُوه ومُنِّ وَمَّد حجَمُا مُومْا.

كُه حِمِ حُجْخا واُموزُا وَمُومُوِّ مَى لَمُجُاوءاُا.

حمُبْرَم وَرِجُوز مُبْرَم وُجُا هُا حمَّىَّقُا حُه:

230   So that through the allegories, it might learn the symbols of the
            crucifixion.
       "Choose a heifer and let the priest take it out from the [camp of
            the] nation."
       If it was not a symbol, why did he bring it out from the nation?
       Let him slaughter it inside the camp: then it will [still] be a sac-
            rifice!
       But because it was a symbol, he took it[43] and went out, apart
            from the nation.
235   It was the likeness of our Lord whom the priests and the
            Sadducees brought out,
       who would be a sacrifice on behalf of sinners, outside of the na-
            tion.[44]
       The teachers of the people led Him out of Jerusalem,[45]
       and they slaughtered Him outside that He might be the purifica-
            tion of the world.[46]
       He carried with Him the wood of the cross when He went out
            [of the city],

---

[43] O: ܘܢܣܒ, "He took it." The Bedjan text reads, ܘܢܣܒܗ, "he took her."

[44] L: ܠܥܡܐ ܠܒܪ ܡܢ ܓܓܘܠܬܐ "who would be a sacrifice on
Golgotha, outside of the nation."

[45] All four Gospels are clear that Jesus was led out of the city and exe-
cuted by the Roman authorities. Mar Jacob, as with all other church
writers during the patristic age, places the responsibility of Jesus' death
at the hands of the Jewish leaders who delivered Him to the Romans.
Hence why this stanza describes the Jewish teachers as being the ones
leading Jesus out of the city and executing Him. See Matthew 27:31–
35; Mark 15:20–24; Luke 23:25–33; John 19:16–18.

[46] See Hebrews 13:11–12. See also Acts 13:27–29; 1 Thessalonians
2:14–15.

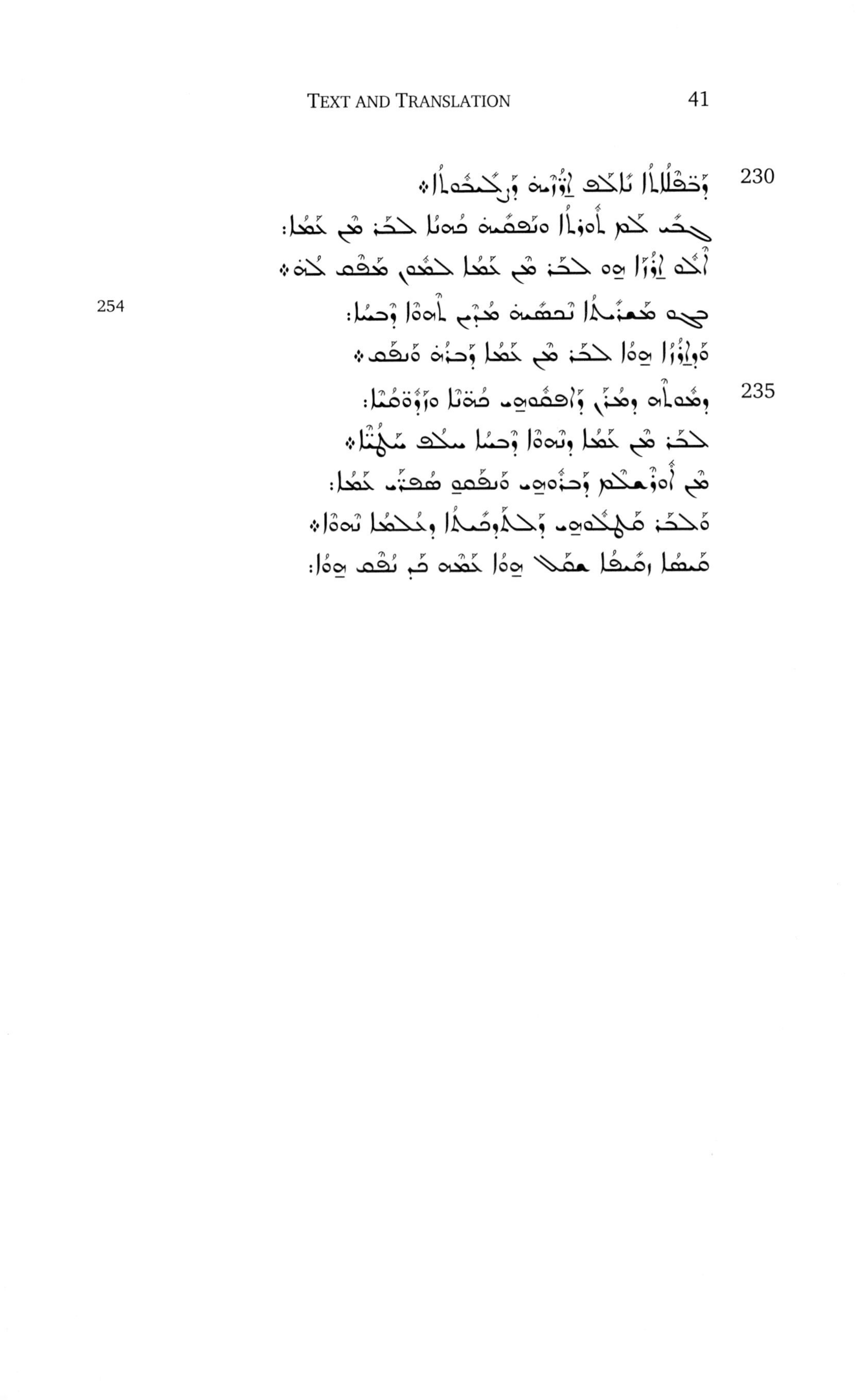

240   just as the cedarwood which Moses brought out for the sacrifice.
The body of the Great Savior was spotted[47] by the blood of the
    scourges,
just like the color[48] of that sacrifice of Moses which was red.
The defiled ones crucified Him who purifies the entire world.
The priest too who slew[49] the heifer became defiled.
245   His forgiving blood flowed from His side on Golgotha,
and it fulfilled in its color the place of the scarlet dye.
Water along with blood went out from the Savior,
for the sacrifice was also thrown into water to purify the defiled
    ones.
Our Lord alone purified the unclean ones from defilement,
250   for He is the sprinkling suitable for the purification of the
    unclean ones.
He is the great remedy for the scars of all who fell,
and there is no ulcer which He healed that resists Him.
Come, O Jew, and see the sprinkling of the Church today,
which purifies the defiled without the ashes of the heifer.
255   She carries the cross instead of that wool of scarlet.
She seals the defiled ones and they are purified of their blemish-
    es.
She carries the body and the blood and sprinkles the wounds,
and through it [= the cross], all the stains[50] of every sinner are
    whitened.
She sprinkled some of it on harlots who are not holy,

---

[47] L: ܐܠܝ, "poured out."

[48] L: ܓܘܢܐ

[49] O: ܢܟܣܗ

[50] O: ܘܡܚܘܪܝܢ ܟܠ ܗܘ ܡܘܡܐ ܕܟܠ ܚܛܝܐ ܒܗ "and through her, all the scars of every sinner are whitened."

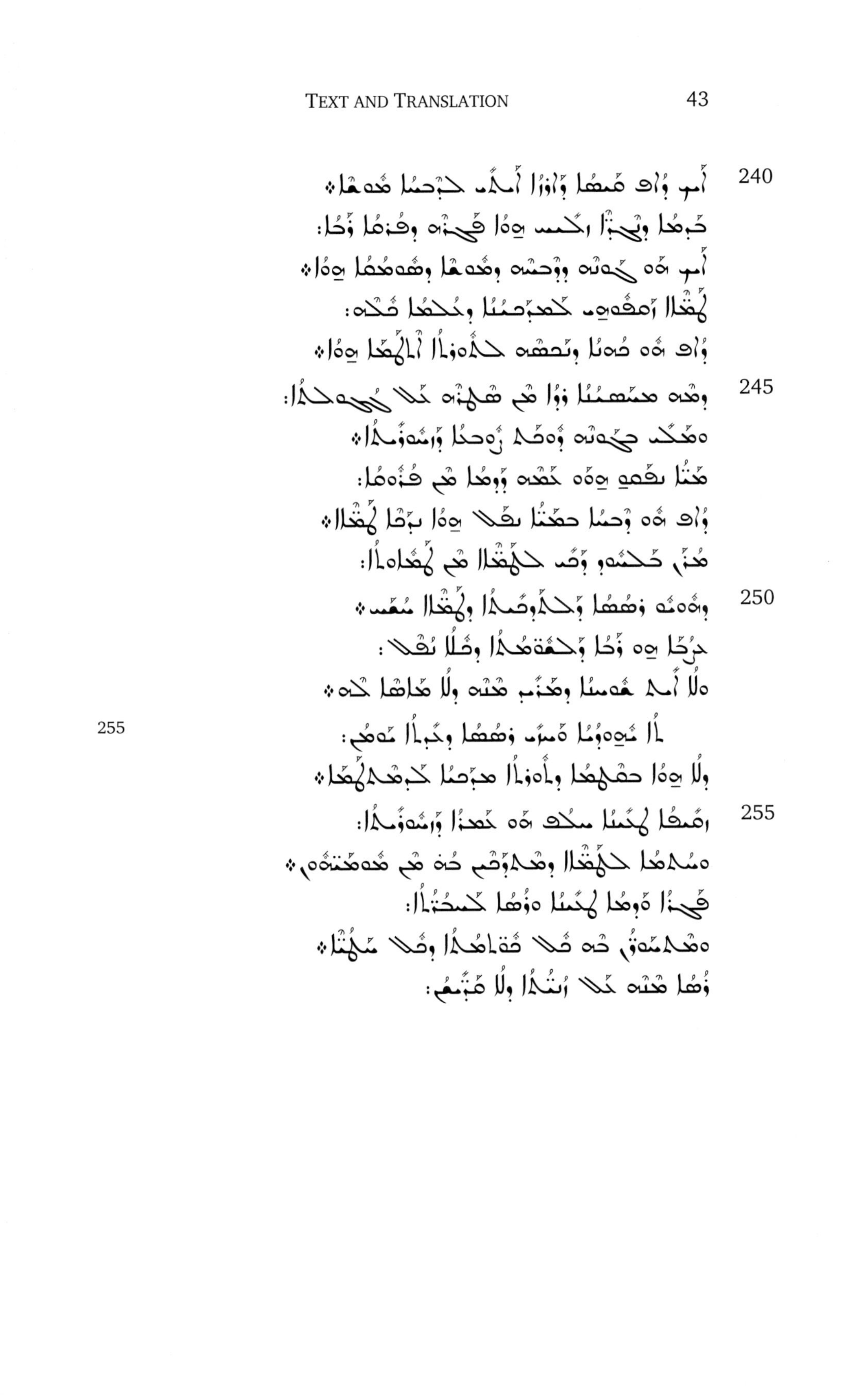

260   and through the water they became virgins in some sacred
              manner.[51]
       This sprinkling fell[52] upon the Publican and he was set aright,[53]
       and it placed the sinful woman in the rank of the Apostles.[54]
       A trickle of it went to the thief, an avid wolf,
       and it made him a lamb that he would enter and graze in the
              Kingdom.[55]
265   If this sprinkling is sprinkled on an old man,
       he would become a youth through the spiritual second birth.[56]
       This sprinkling purifies the soul from defilement.
       O you who are defiled! Come, whiten with it your blemishes![57]
       Through this symbol, Moses purified the children of his nation.
270   There was no power in the heifer to purify anything.
       The beauty of the likeness of our Lord poured forth[58] over the
              Hebrew people,
       and through it, the defiled ones of the nation were truly puri-
              fied.
       Through the color of the heifer and that of the scarlet dye,[59]
       the Law clearly portrayed the blood of the Savior.[60]

---

[51] See Luke 7:36–50; John 4:1–42; John 8:1–11.

[52] L: ܣܪ "was sprinkled."

[53] See Matthew 9:9–13; Luke 18:9–14.

[54] L: ܕܥܠܝ̈ܡܬܐ, "of the maidens." In Syriac texts, the sinful woman regularly refers to the anonymous woman of Luke 7. See Luke 7:36–50.

[55] See Luke 23:32–43.

[56] See John 3:1–8.

[57] See Psalm 51:7; Isaiah 1:18.

[58] L: ܐܬܠ "poured out."

[59] L: ܓܘܢܐ "color."

[60] L: ܦܪܘܩܐ

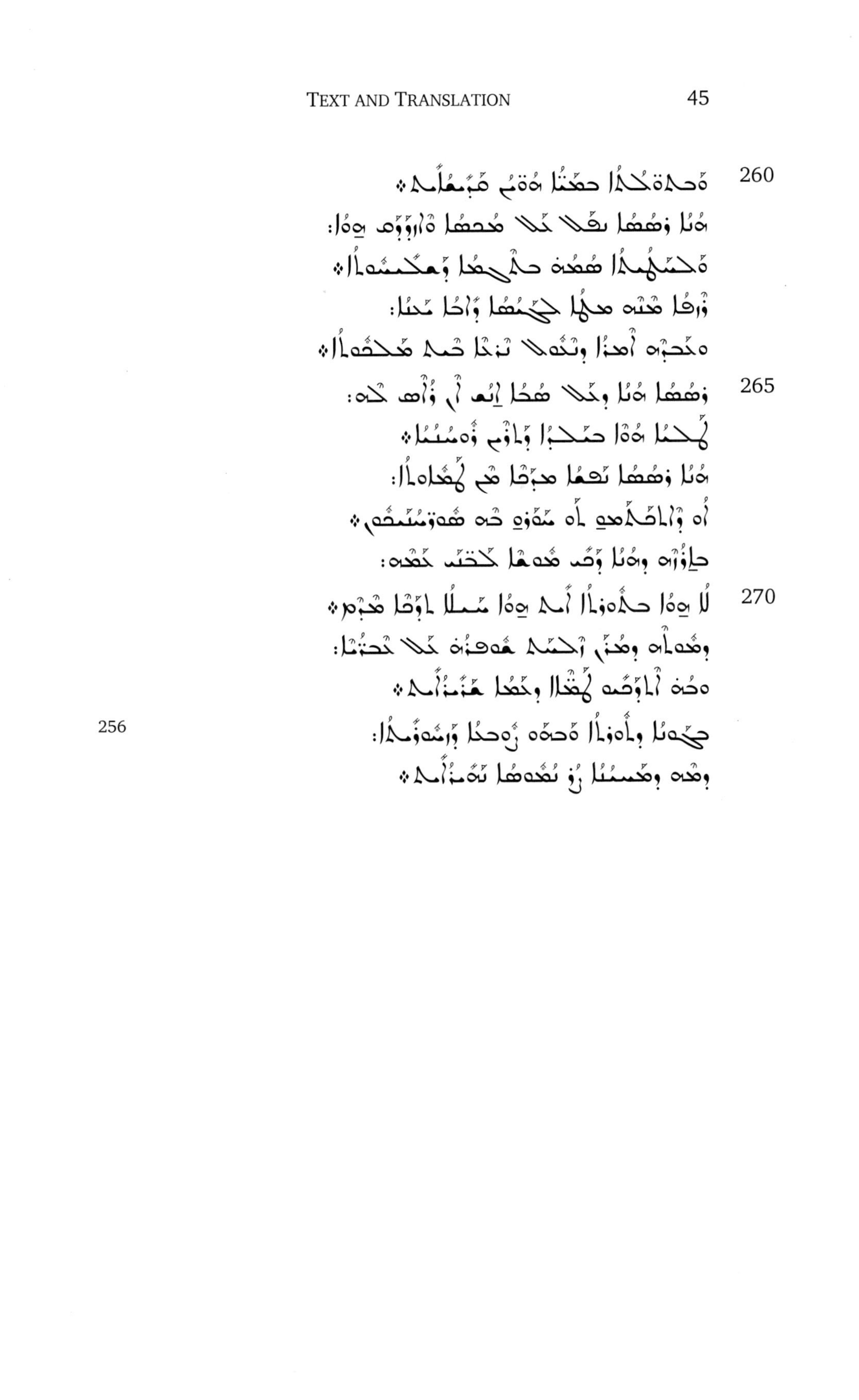

256

275   The priest with his finger sprinkled blood in the Tabernacle,
     to instruct the soul to seal its gates[61] through the atoning blood.
     "Sprinkle seven times towards the Tabernacle
     from the blood of the heifer," he commanded the priest who
         slayed her.
     Moses hinted to you if you look clearly,
280   for there are seven gates[62] in your being which you seal[63]
         through blood.
     Let the cross be a guardian for the gate of the soul,
     that it may be shut[64] before the stranger so that he will not enter
         it.
     He instructed you through the wool for it carried the color of
         the scarlet,
     to dye your soul with God to acquire His color.
285   Let love kindle the burning sacrifice that will burn iniquity.
     Kindle your soul to God through tears of love.
     O that I might be given love that will hear clearly,
     so that the symbol of Moses might be uttered again abundantly.
     Its beauty stirs me to redouble my word on the reading,
290   that the beauty of the image which was entirely marvellous will
         be made manifest again.
     His book gestured to me: Read me clearly
     and then you will find great wealth amongst my verses.
     O intelligent ones, give me your hearing with love,
     that through the parable[65] of Moses we may prudently grow
         rich.

---

[61] O: ܐܢܬܗ "its gate."

[62] O: ܐܢܬܠܐ

[63] O: ܚܬܡ "[which] seals."

[64] O: ܐܢܣܝܐ

[65] O: ܒܦܠܐܬܗ "that through the parables."

حمحمحمِرحلا حُمدلا حرُحﻟه ﻭحُا وُّاهﻪ ﻭﻩُﻟ: 275

ﻭﻧكلﻘﻪ حلَﻘحا ﻭﻟسدُﻩﻩم لُﻭﻧ̇مه حُرحُا مَﻬسا۔

محﻛ زَﺣﺘكﻟﻟ ﻭُﻩﻪ كلم كُﻩمحلا مَﻩمحﻣِﺣﻟا:

مَﻪ ﻭحُﻩﻪ ﻭلُﻩﻭﻟ̇ا قَﻘﺐ حلحُﻩﻧلا ﻭﻧُﺛﺔ ﻭﻩﻟ كﻟﺔ۔

ﻭﻩُم كلﺮ مُﻩمﻬﻟ لُ سلُﻭ لُﻳﻟ ﻧَﻩَﻣﻧ̇ﺎﻟﻪ:

ﻭمَﺣﺣﻟ لُﻭﻧ̇حﺮ ﻭُلﻪ محﻣﻭمحﺮ حُرحُا لسدُﻩﻩم۔ 280

حلﻭُحُﻟ ﻭﻧﻠﺤﺎ رِحﺤﻟ ﻧﻩﻩﻟ حﺤﺮ ﻧُﻬﻭﻭُﻟ:

ﻭﻟﻩﻩﻟ لُسﺮﻟ حﺮُم ﻧَﻭحُﻧُﻟ ﻭلا ﻧﺛﻩﻟ كﻟﺔ۔

حﻧﻘﺣﻧُا لُﺣﻘﺐ ﻭحﻘحلا ﻳُﻩﻧﺔ ﻭﺮﻧﺷﻭﻭُمﻛﻟ:

لُﺮﻘﻩﻩ ﻧﻘحﺮ لُﻳﻟ حلﺤﻟ̇ﺎ مﻳﻩﻧﺔ لُﻣﻧﻟا۔

ﻭﻧُﻘﺐ ﻭﺣﺤﻟ لُﻭحل ﺷﻭحُﻟ ﻭحﻠلا ﻧُﻟحﺐ: 285

حﺮُﺣﻧﻟ ﻭﺷﻭحُﻟ مﻳﻩﻭﻧﺔ حلﻘحﺮ زِﺮ لُحﻟﺔﻟ۔

مَﺮ ﻭﺑ ﻧﻭﻭ كﺮ ﺷﻭحُﻟ ﻭﻟﻘحﺐ ﻧﻩَﻣﻧﺌﺎﻟﻪ:

ﻭلُﻭﺕ ﻧﻟﻩحﺤلا لُﻭﺮﻩ ﻭمُﻩﻣﻬﻟ حلﻛَﻣﻧﺌﺎﻟﻪ۔

ﻳَﻧﺮﺤﻳﺮ مُﻩﻘﻧﺔ لُﻧﻭﻩ محكلﺮ حلا ﻗﻧُﻣﻟا:

ﻭلُﻭﺕ ﻧﻟﻩﻣﻧﻩﻟ مُﻩﻘﻧﺔ ﻭرِﺤﺤﻟ ﻭﺛﻛﺔ لُﻭﻭُﻟ ﻩﻩ۔ 290

حلُﻛﺔﻩ ﻭﻩُم كﺮ ﻭحﺮُﺛ حﺮ كلم ﻧﻩَﻣﻧﺌﺎﻟﻪ:

ﻩلُﻭﺕ مَﻘحﺮ لُﻳﻟ حﺣﻧلا مﻘﻩحﺐ مُﻩلُﻭُﻟ ﻭُحلا۔

ﻩَﻭﺟ كﺮ رِﻩلُﻟ لُﻩ قﻧُﻩﻣﻬﻟ مَﺤﻣحﻛﺄﻟﻪ:

ﻭُﻭﻘلﻟلُﻟﻩ ﻭمُﻩﻣﻬﻟ ﻧﺤكُﻭ قﻧُﻩﻣﻬلﺔ۔

295 Why and for what reason was the heifer burned in fire,
  if not to depict a type of the bread of the Son of God?
  In the conflagration of the sacrifice which was made, the Eucharistic bread was represented,
  for it also burns in fire to purify the one who takes it.
  The Law commanded that they should cast the sacrifice in a place that was purified;
300 the place that is purified it called the church for it is a house of propitiation.
  The bread of our Lord is made a purification for the entire world,
  that the church divides affectionately for her children.
  Come, O nations of the earth! Become pure through this sprinkling!
  For there is power in it that will also cure the wounds of the soul.[66]
305 If through the hand of Moses, His shadow purified the people,
  how much more through His substance will He give life to those invoking Him?
  If a person from the nation came close to the bone of a dead person,
  they sprinkled him from the conflagration of the heifer.
  Thus, if your person dies altogether today,
310 the church has a sprinkling that gives you life, if you desire.
  She does not purify you through the blood of calves which you offer,
  nor does she sprinkle the ashes of the heifer on your wounds.
  She does not bring you cedarwood to whiten yourself by it,
  neither through the wool of the scarlet does she cleanse your iniquity.

---

[66] See Hebrews 9:11–14.

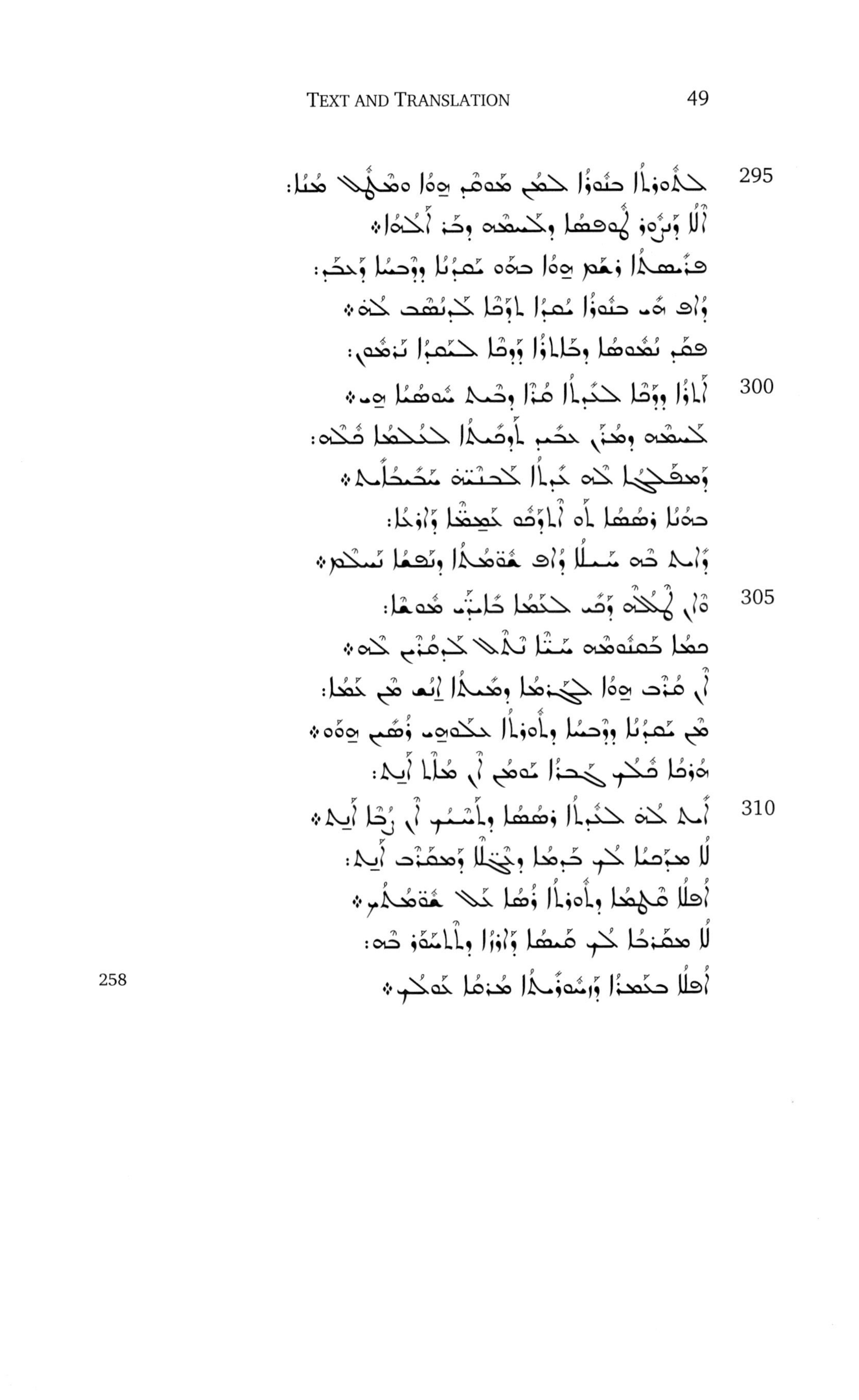

315   She neither sprinkles on you water with the hyssop from the
            conflagration,
        nor does she make you stink by the blood of the various sacri-
            fices.[67]
        She makes the sign of the cross which is the summation of all
            sacrifices,
        and through it, she gives you everlasting light and life.[68]
        Come out, O Jew, from the shadows which you serve,
320   and come, be completely enlightened by the cross of light which
            you do not love!
        You are exempt[69] of sacrifices; the church[70] does not require
            bulls from you.
        Come in person – there is a sacrifice that purifies you!
        No one requires you to bring tithes with you,
        and there are no offerings[71] except your own person to God.
325   If you come, do not bring a heifer to us to sacrifice.
        Come and become whitened by the crucifixion and blot out your
            iniquity.
        If your soul is red like the scarlet in iniquity,
        the cross will whiten and purify it[72] from defilement.
        If you are more defiled[73] than the scarlet dye,

---

[67] L: ܕܕܒܚܢ̈ "sacrifices." The Bedjan text shows ܕܕܒܚ "sacrifice" which was
rendered as a plural above for the sake of the English translation. The
translation would have read literally: "nor does it make you stink by
the blood of the sacrifice of the various kinds."
[68] See Ephesians 2:13–18; Colossians 1:19–22; 2:13–15.
[69] O: ܣܛܘܡ "Exempt [yourself]."
[70] Sic O: ܒܥܕܬ
[71] O: ܩܘܪܒܢܐ "offering."
[72] L: ܠܟ "you."
[73] L: ܬܚܫܟܝܢ "you will be darkened."

315 لَا وُهُا حكَحبِ هَنْنُا دَوهُا هَي هَعبُنُا:

ولَا هدَوههُا كبِ كبِهُا ووحمُا وهَبِو هَبِو ❖

رَهَحُا وُحعُا وهُوهُه هُحُا وحَحَوَهِ وَحَنْا:

وحُه هُوحُا كبِ نُوهوُا وهَنْا ولَا هُوكحُا ❖

قُوه نُوووُنُا هَي لِنُخِلَا وَهعهُعِه أَبِه:

320 وأَا بَوَ هُكبِ حَبِكَِد نُوهوُا ولَا وُشِم أَبِه ❖

محَبِ أَبِه وَحَنْا لَا حُحُا كبِ هَبِأَا أَووُا:

حنَحهُبِ أَا كبِ أَبِه بِوَه وَحمُا وَهمَحهُا كبِ ❖

كه هَحهعَتَا حُنَا كبِ إِنَه أَبِأَا هَهُبِ:

ولَا هُوتحُنَا أَلَا هنُوهبِ زِبِ أَكحهُا ❖

325 لَا أَبِأَا كِ أَوزِأَا حَبِحمُا أَ أَلَا أَبِه:

حَبِكَحهُا لَا أَاهَهَو هَحهَ هَوكبِ ❖

أَ هُوهُحُا حنَهلَا نَحهُبِ أَبِ أَوَكحهُا:

رَهَحُا همَهَو هَهمَحلَا كَه هَي لِهَهوا أَا ❖

أَ أَاحَهَم لِحه هَي نُوحُا وَرَمَوَهِأَا:

330   the death of the Son will purify you, if you will confess Him.
Moses also purified you mystically through our Lord,
and through Him all those sacrifices which were offered were
        received.
Leave the sacrifice and offer yourself to God,
for it is not something belonging to you that He wants but you
        yourself.
335   There is the sacrifice that you crucified which purifies you.
Cleanse yourself of His killing and He will atone you of your
        debts.
If the Father of truth is loved by you, confess His Son.
And if you love the whole-burnt sacrifices, He is also the sacri-
        fice.
If you seek the purification of the soul, He purifies you.
340   And if you desire the sprinkling, He sprinkles on you His blood.
You do not abolish the Law on account of Him if you love Him;
all sacrifices are comprised in Him without the stench.
He is Pontiff and Sacrifice and Priest[74] and the One who
        atones.[75]
Blessed is He through whose symbols Moses purified the entire
        nation.

---

[74] L: ܗܘܣ ܘܩܪܘܒܐ ܘܩܕܡ ܘܟܗܢܐ ܘܡܚܣܝܢܐ "He is Pontiff and Priest and Sacrifice, and the One who atones."
[75] See Hebrews 2:17; 3:1–2; 4:14–15; 5:1–10; 6:20; 7:26–28; 8:1–7;
9:11–28.

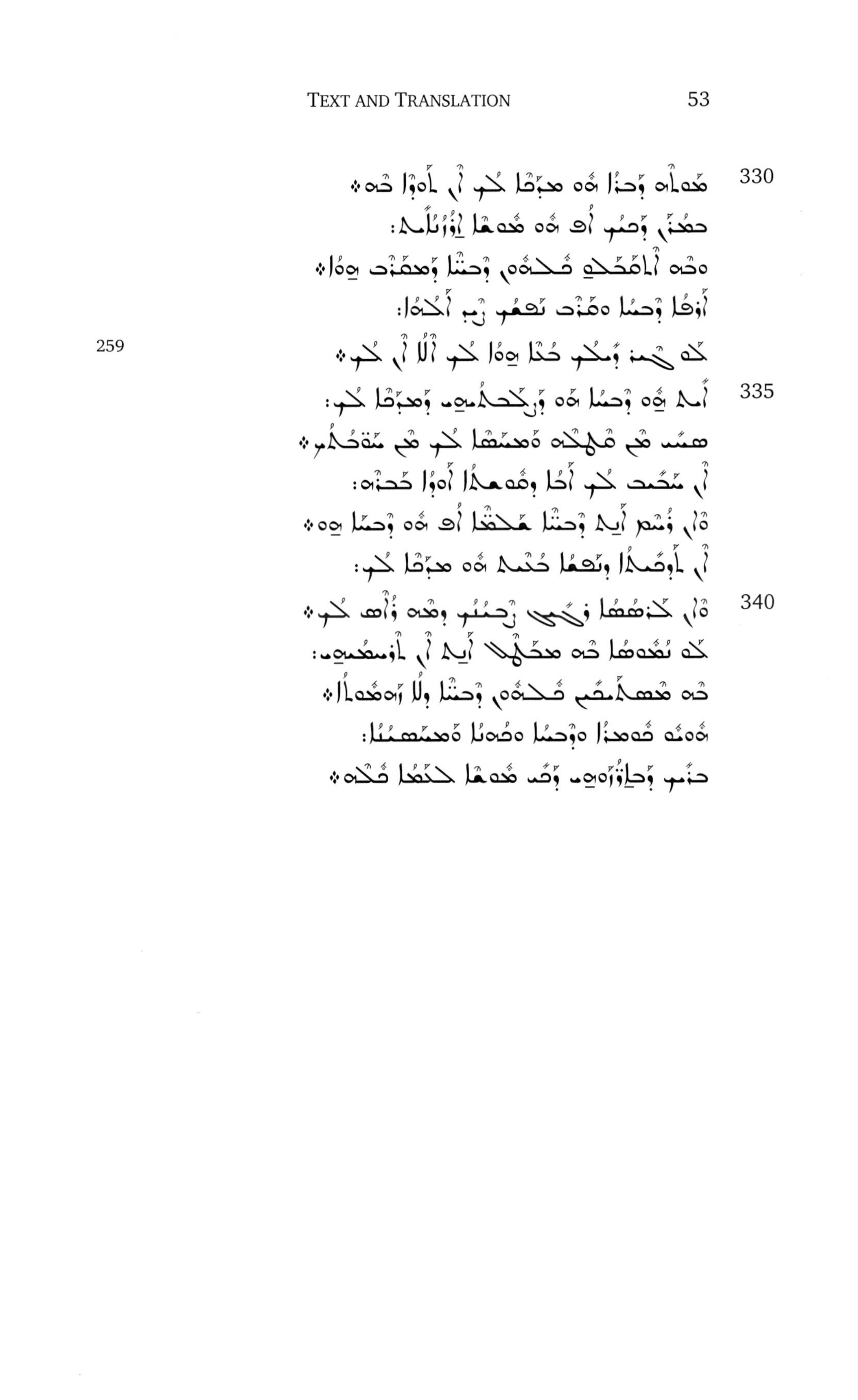

259

BIBLIOGRAPHY

ANCIENT SOURCES

Bedjan, Paulus, ed. *Homiliae selectae Mar-Jacobi Sarugensis*, I–V. Paris–Leipzig: Otto Harrassowitz, 1902–1910. Reprinted as *Homilies of Mar Jacob of Sarug*, I–VI. Piscataway: Gorgias Press, 2006.

Patrologia Graeca. Edited by J.-P. Migne. 161 vols. Paris, 1857–1886.

MODERN SOURCES

Brock, Sebastian P. "Baptismal Themes in the writings of Jacob of Serug." Pages 325–47 in *Symposium Syriacum*. Vol. 205 of *Orientalia Christiana Analecta*. Edited by François Graffin and Antoine Guillaumont. Rome: Pontificium Institutum Orientalium Studiorum, 1978.

———. "Some Important Baptismal Themes in the Syriac Tradition." *Harp* 4 (1991): 189–214.

———. "Fire from Heaven: from Abel's Sacrifice to the Eucharist." Pages 229–243 in *Fire from Heaven: Studies in Syriac Theology and Liturgy*. Vol. 25 of *Studia Patristica: Biblica et Apocrypha, Orientalia, Ascetica*. Edited by Amy Livingstone. Leuven: Peeters Publishers, 1993. Reprinted in Vol. 863 of *Variorum Collected Studies Series*. London: Ashgate Variorum, 2006.

Harrak, Amir, trans. *Jacob of Sarug's Homily on the Partaking of the Holy Mysteries*. Vol. 19 of *Texts from Christian Late An-*

tiquity. Edited by George A. Kiraz. Piscataway: Gorgias Press, 2013.

Kaplan, Aryeh. *Sefer Yetzirah: The Book of Creation*. Rev. ed. Boston: Weiser Books, 1997.

Lane, David J. "Jacob of Sarug: On the Red Heifer." *Harp* 15 (2002), 25–42.

Lehto, Adam. *The Demonstrations of Aphrahat, the Persian Sage*. Vol. 27 of *Gorgias Eastern Christian Studies*. Edited by George A. Kiraz, István Perczel, Lorenzo Perrone, and Samuel Rubenson. Piscataway: Gorgias Press, 2010.

Wickes, Jeffrey T., trans. *St. Ephrem the Syrian: The Hymns on Faith*. Vol. 130 of *The Fathers of the Church: A New Translation*. Edited by David G. Hunter et al. Washington: The Catholic University of America Press, 2015.

Index of Biblical References

References are to line number